ON TOCQUEVILLE

ALSO BY ALAN RYAN

ON TOCQUEVILLE

Democracy and America

ALAN RYAN

LIVERIGHT PUBLISHING CORPORATION

A Division of W. W. Norton & Company
New York / London

CONTENTS

PREFACE

In the introduction to *On Politics*, I suggested that one measure of the book's success would be the readers who went and read the works of the authors I discussed. Some readers suggested that I might encourage them to do so by taking chapters of *On Politics* and adding to them substantial extracts from the works I hoped they would read. What follows is exactly that, with a short introduction to provide some of the context that the chapter's original placement in *On Politics* would have provided. As before, I am grateful to Bob Weil and William Menaker at Liveright, as well as to the Norton production team, for their help in making an author's life as easy as it can plausibly be made.

CHRONOLOGY

1607   Jamestown settlement, Virginia

1620   New Plymouth Colony, New England

1642–47   English Civil War

1685   Revocation of Edict of Nantes; end of toleration
            of Protestants in France

1688–89   The Glorious Revolution; Declaration and Bill
            of Rights issued

1689   Birth of Charles-Louis de Secondat, Baron de la
            Brède et de Montesquieu

1712   Birth of Jean-Jacques Rousseau at Geneva

1715   Death of Louis XIV

1721   Montesquieu publishes *Persian Letters*
            (anonymously)

1728   Rousseau leaves Geneva

1729   Montesquieu visits England

1748   Montesquieu publishes *The Spirit of the Laws*

1750   Rousseau publishes *Discourse on the Arts and Sciences*

1751	*The Spirit of the Laws* placed on the Index of prohibited books
1755	Death of Montesquieu; Rousseau publishes *Discourse on the Origin of Inequality*
1761	Rousseau publishes *La nouvelle Héloïse*
1762	Rousseau publishes *Social Contract* and *Émile*
1767	Birth of Benjamin Constant
1775	Revolutionary War begins
1776	Declaration of Independence
1778	Death of Rousseau
1783	Treaty of Paris ends Revolutionary War
1787	Constitutional Convention produces American Constitution
1789	Fall of the Bastille; commencement of French Revolution
1792	France is declared a republic
1793	The Terror begins in France; execution of Louis XVI
1794	Imprisonment of Tocqueville's parents; they are sentenced to death, but released after Robespierre's fall in July
1795	Revised constitution, with restricted suffrage, bicameral legislature, and Directory, a five-person executive
1799	Napoleon overthrows the Directory and seizes power as first consul
1804	Napoleon crowns himself emperor
1805	Birth of Alexis de Tocqueville

1815	Battle of Waterloo; exile of Napoleon; restoration of the Bourbon monarchy
1819	Constant delivers his lecture "The Liberty of the Ancients Compared with That of the Moderns"
1830	July Revolution; abdication of Charles X; death of Constant; accession of Louis-Philippe
1831–32	Tocqueville and Gustave de Beaumont travel in America (May 11–February 20)
1833	Publication of *Du système pénitentiaire aux États-Unis*; Tocqueville's first visit to England
1835	Publication of *Democracy in America*, volume 1; Tocqueville's second visit to England
1839	Tocqueville elected to Chamber of Deputies
1840	Publication of *Democracy in America*, volume 2
1841	Tocqueville's first journey to Algeria; Tocqueville elected to the Académie Française
1848	February Revolution; Tocqueville elected to Constituent Assembly; serves briefly as foreign minister under Louis Napoleon; Louis Napoleon elected president of the Second Republic in December
1851	Louis Napoleon's coup d'état; Tocqueville briefly imprisoned
1856	Death of Hervé, Tocqueville's father; Tocqueville publishes *L'ancien régime et la révolution*
1859	Tocqueville dies of tuberculosis in Cannes; buried in his Normandy château

INTRODUCTION

❧

THE DISCUSSION OF TOCQUEVILLE that follows these introductory pages has been taken from a long book, *On Politics*. In that setting, it was preceded and followed by chapters on particular thinkers and ideas that gave it a context in a longer argument that provided the thread on which the discussions hung. The longer argument was about the possibility of self-government. Can human beings govern themselves, or are they the playthings of fate, or helplessly at the mercy of irrational drives that they neither comprehend nor know how to control? If self-government is possible, how is it to be accomplished? Is the price of a whole society's being self-governing a degree of discipline for the members of that society that makes individual self-government, or individual liberty, always the enemy of collective self-government? Is individual autonomy the enemy of the autonomy of a political community?

Spartans prized their political self-government so highly that they would die to the last man to defend it; but individual liberty was nonexistent. Tocqueville is one of several thinkers in the nineteenth and twentieth centuries who pointed to a paradox in the modern search for freedom. Liberal democracies set out to solve the ancient problem of reconciling individual and collective self-government, but the experience of individuals in democracies is that we do not "rule ourselves" but find ourselves ruled by everyone else. In emphasizing the role of the "tyranny of opinion" in a democratic society, Tocqueville introduced a new anxiety to modern social and political thought—that each of us would be governed by forces that worked on our psyches rather than our bodies, that political self-government would turn into the management of a "flock of industrious animals," not citizens but sheep. The discussion of contemporary democracy in *On Politics* suggested that Tocqueville's anxieties were exaggerated but not absurd; modern Americans are notably un-sheep-like, but by Tocqueville's standards they have done better at sustaining varied and interesting lives as consumers than as citizens.

When Alexis de Tocqueville sent John Stuart Mill a copy of his work on the antecedents of the French Revolution, *L'ancien régime et la révolution*, Mill responded that Tocqueville had now produced three masterpieces: the two volumes of *Democracy in America*, so different in style and tone, constituted two distinct masterpieces rather than two parts of one only. A good deal of Tocqueville's impact on Mill stemmed from the fact that even before the first volume of *Democracy* appeared in 1835, Mill had become convinced that a new kind of political science was needed to make sense of the rapidly changing society and politics of the early nineteenth century. One of Tocqueville's most striking claims in *Democracy* was that "equality of condition," the phenomenon that he identified with the "democratic" quality of American society, demanded a new political science for its understanding.

Mill thought that Tocqueville had indeed provided a new political science, not in the twentieth-century sense of a discipline built on opinion surveys and complex statistical analysis, but in a somewhat older sense, that of a new way of conceptualizing and understanding the political world. What Tocqueville offered was an exemplary analysis that provided a historical and (to adopt the word that August Comte had just coined) sociological account of how American institutions had come to be the way they were, rooted in a deep understanding of human nature, the universal qualities of individuals on which the processes of socialization had to work to produce Frenchmen and Americans. The one truly universal science of man was psychology; the social sciences studied mankind in different historical and political contexts. Mill hoped at this time to contribute to the creation of a discipline that he called "ethology," in modern terms the theory of socialization. Political scientists today study political socialization, and everyone concerned with education would like to be better informed about how upbringing turns, or ideally can turn, infant raw material into knowledgeable and cooperative adults.

If Tocqueville had produced a new political science, it was as a gifted sociologist and political scientist, not as a philosopher. Mill was already contemplating writing a philosophical treatise on logic and the philosophy of scientific inquiry when he encountered the first volume of *Democracy in America*. *A System of Logic* appeared in 1843, three years after the second volume of *Democracy in America*, and the sixth book—"On the Logic of the Moral Sciences"—was in many ways the destination toward which the earlier discussions of formal logic, the nature of proof in the natural sciences, the nature of causal laws, and much else had been steering all along. "Moral sciences" was the eighteenth- and nineteenth-century term for all those inquiries in which the properties of the human mind played a causal role: what we now know as psychology and the social sciences. Mill was only one of many critics who turned *Democracy in America* to their own purposes; and these purposes differed widely. In the United States itself, Catharine Beecher, the sister of Harriet Beecher Stowe, the author of *Uncle Tom's Cabin*, and of Henry Ward Beecher the famous preacher, drew on Tocqueville's account of the role of women in American life to challenge the early advocates of female suffrage and defend her own ideal of "republican motherhood." A woman's role was to bring up her family in strong Christian principles, which were, she argued in *Domestic Economy*, the very principles of American democracy. Mill, the agnostic author of *The Subjection of Women*, was not likely to be convinced.

It is the fate of books to be turned to whatever uses their readers have in mind, but Tocqueville did not write in a vacuum, nor were his ideas wholly novel. There are three thinkers who play a not very explicit role in *Democracy in America*, although they figure in Tocqueville's letters and in his biography, and this brief introduction will provide a sketch of the ideas that Tocqueville took to America, accepting some and rejecting others. A fourth thinker—Benjamin Constant—provides perhaps the most useful framework in which to situate liberals of Tocqueville's stamp. Although they are discussed chronologically, in some ways the first of them provided Tocqueville with his most important ideas. This is Montesquieu, whose *Spirit of the Laws*, published in 1748, has some claim to be the founding work of what we now understand as political sociology, though there are many other claimants to the title, stretching all the way back to Aristotle. In terms of the way we think about societies that we see as distinctively modern and liberal, however, it is Montesquieu who provides our starting point. When Montesquieu discusses the "spirit" of the laws, he disavows an intention to explore familiar distinctions between public and private law, or constitutional law and more ordinary law. *The Spirit of the Laws* is a sprawling, unsummarizable, work, but whatever else it is, it is an exploration of the political cultures of different political systems. Montesquieu employs something other than the familiar distinction between monarchies, aristocracies, and democracies, government by the one, the few, and the many, and their bad mirror images, tyranny, oligarchy, and ochlocracy or mob rule. The reason is a concern that permeates *Democracy in America* eighty years later: How can moderate government be preserved? Moderate government was in essence what the founding fathers of the United States attempted to create with their innovative federal constitution for their newly independent country. It allows for the expression of a wide diversity of opinions and interests, and attempts to combine the virtues of monarchy, aristocracy, and democracy in a mixed form of government, under the rule of law and minimizing the scope for the exercise of mere arbitrary power.

Of Montesquieu's innumerable concerns, three matter here. One was to distinguish monarchy, even absolute monarchy as practiced in France, from mere despotism such as he thought characterized the Ottoman Empire. This was where the notion of the "spirit" of the laws played a role. The animating principle, if that is the word, of the Ottoman or any other despotic system is fear. The sole ruler is master of the persons and possessions of all his subjects, and may destroy them at his pleasure. He may for the most part leave his subjects to their own devices, as many writers have suggested that the rulers of the Ottoman Empire largely did; but they have no right to be left to their own devices, and no remedies if they suffer persecution or abuse. Of course, in practice a number of checks on the despot's power will always exist; as David Hume pointed out, all political authority rests on consent to the extent that a tyrant needs willing servants to ensure that his less willing subjects remain obedient. What there is not is a system of rules, or laws, on which his authority rests, and which give his subjects some confidence that they will not suffer arbitrary ill-use.

A monarchy rests on the principle of honor. Political authority hangs on status, and the monarch's own security depends on his acceptability to the aristocratic hierarchy at the top of which he stands. It is, of course, the French monarchy that Montesquieu had in mind, as did Tocqueville, the future author of *L'ancien régime*. If distinguishing the French monarchy, a moderate regime even if constitutionally absolute, was one task, a second was to explain the peculiarities of the British monarchy. For Britain, though a monarchy, was animated by freedom rather than, or perhaps as well as, by honor. This was an effect of the British commitment to the separation of powers, a concept that Montesquieu put into circulation without ever being entirely specific about just what it involved. The notion that the legislative, executive, and judicial branches of government could be "separate" in the rigid fashion required by the U.S. Constitution was at odds with a parliamentary system in which the king's ministers sat in parliament, as did the "law lords." Crucially, however, there was an independent judiciary, whose members held their posts during good behavior, and nobody could be deprived of his or her liberty or property other than according to law. The British therefore possessed guarantees of personal liberty and control over their own property that the French did not. A Frenchman might find himself in the Bastille under a *lettre de cachet*, a warrant for his detention without trial, with no formal avenue of appeal. Since the Glorious Revolution, no such thing was possible in Britain. Moreover, the British monarchy rested on a more solid foundation than the French, because Britain was a pluralistic society that required the gentry to exercise all manner of local legal and political functions, with a representative assembly in the shape of a parliament whose assent to taxation was essential, and which was the source of statute law. The French monarchy had systematically centralized all authority in the royal court at Versailles, meaning that the aristocracy possessed privileges unjustified by the performing of useful administrative and political tasks. This was to undermine the foundations of monarchy and aristocracy alike. The absence of representative institutions also deprived the French monarchy of valuable information about public opinion, for which the well-meant investigations of the crown's local officials was no substitute.

The third of Montesquieu's concerns was the contrast between the world of the ancient city-states such as Athens and Sparta and the modern world of the nation-state. Could modern men—Montesquieu was a sensitive observer of the lives of women, but ancient republics were a male arena—live up to the standards of their Greek and Roman ancestors? Montesquieu thought not, not because modern man was too corrupt to feel the ardent patriotism of the Athenians at Marathon, but because modern states were too large and too complex. City-states were maintained by "virtue"—as opposed to the fear that underpinned despotisms—which in this context meant something quite other than

Christian virtue, rather the capacity for self-sacrifice, military endurance, and uninterest in financial success. Modern societies were commercial. In commercial societies, we pursue our interests, rationally, peaceably, and with a view to our long-term prosperity. Commerce is intrinsically "gentle," whereas ancient city-states, constantly at war or on the verge of war, were almost necessarily committed to the military virtues; commerce requires us to persuade others to accept what we have to trade and requires them to persuade us to accept what they have to exchange. Persuasion is at the opposite extreme from warfare aimed at the forcible acquisition of loot.

The attractions of commercial society were almost wholly lost on Rousseau, the second of the influences on Tocqueville. But Rousseau's critique of commercial society has struck a chord with enormous numbers of readers down to the present day. Contrary to most readers' first impressions, Rousseau was not in the modern sense a democrat, but he was deeply committed to the idea that political authority must rest on the consent of all citizens. Law, at any rate the fundamental laws of a society, must be an emanation of the general will in order to be legitimate. The general will is simultaneously the will of the collectivity and the will of each person when he—no more than the Spartans whom he admired did Rousseau propose that women should form an active part of the citizen body—asks himself what is in the long-run interests of every member of the society, considered impartially. The concept of the general will is one that has caused innumerable disputes in subsequent political discussion; the fiercest critics think the idea of a collective will is both nonsensical and dangerous, less fierce critics that it is more nearly vacuous.

The importance of Rousseau for our purposes lies less in the complications of the concept of the general will than in his insistence that the general will possesses absolute authority over the citizenry, and his obsession with its indivisibility and infallibility. Allied to his insistence that the general will was the voice of reason, and that a majority that asked the correct question would always be "in the right," we move very swiftly to a picture of a state that has absolute authority over all its members, and where toleration of dissent is unlikely to be a priority. Rousseau, of course, also admired the patriotism and self-sacrificing virtue of the—idealized—Roman or Spartan citizen. Put these ingredients together, and we have the potential for something Rousseau did not wish for or anticipate, which was the French Revolution, and the characteristically French conception of a republic, which was one and indivisible, entitled to the absolute and unswerving loyalty of its citizens, who in turn would have the distinctively republican liberty that consisted in being a part of a self-governing nation that was itself independent of all others and subservient to none.

Rousseau's relationship to the classical republican tradition, in the sense of the tradition of thinking about the establishment and maintenance of the city-states of antiquity, was extremely ambiguous. He shared the classical detestation of servility in the literal sense of being the slave or servant of some other man, but he added to it the distinctively modern, or perhaps post-Reformation Christian, thought that the overwhelming imperative is to obey only ourselves, which is to say to do what we are conscientiously convinced we must do. Rousseau claimed that when we joined a political community governed under the general will, we did not lose our freedom, but gained it; not only was it true that in giving himself to all each man gave himself to none and remained as free as before, but he also gained the moral freedom that came from obedience to a universal law based on reason.

It is easy enough to read Rousseau in ways that make the suggestion that law is the dictate of universal reason less alarming than it may seem at first sight. If we preserve our independent moral judgment, we shall feel morally obliged to obey the law only when it requires something that we would feel morally obliged to do even in the law's absence; if it requires us to do what we morally ought not, which was one of Montesquieu's several accounts of an infringement of liberty by the law, we shall think it has failed to meet the standard that it must meet to be genuinely law. On the other hand, the lesson of dictators infused with the belief that they and they alone embody the true will of the people, and that their opponents are therefore both mad and wicked, is that from Robespierre to Stalin and Pol Pot, terrible things have been done in the name of freedom and reason.

Long before the horrors of the twentieth century led some critics to accuse Rousseau of begetting what they labeled "totalitarian democracy," Benjamin Constant more temperately spelled out what he thought the problem was that Rousseau had bequeathed to his countrymen. In a famous lecture, "Of the Liberty of the Ancients Compared with That of the Moderns," published in 1819, he laid out the crucial contrast, perhaps more clearly and persuasively than Isaiah Berlin did many years later with his *Two Concepts of Liberty*. "Ancient" liberty was a collective possession; it was, in essence, sovereignty. What each individual had was his share of the sovereign authority within his city-state. What no individual had was the sort of individual freedom that was the gift of the modern world: occupational freedom, the right to worship as he or she chose, the right *not* to devote all one's waking thoughts to the service of the republic. Pericles's observation that the Athenians said of a man who "minds his own business" that he "has *no* business here" is exactly what Constant directs his notion of "modern liberty" against. It is important to see that Constant did not think that ancient liberty was not a form of freedom at all; he was sure that it was a valid concept of liberty. It was the liberty of the classical citizen rather than the liberty of the modern individual.

Modern liberty was most securely enjoyed in countries such as Britain and the newly created United States. These were the paradigmatically liberal states of the day. Constant distinguished between the ancient Greek city-states in a way that brought home the comparison he had in mind. Of the Greek states, Athens was the most "modern" in this sense; Athens was a trading state and had a thriving commercial existence. Like Montesquieu, Constant drew a sharp contrast between ancient city-states that were incessantly at war with their neighbors, or on the verge of war, and modern commercial societies that had an interest in peace and prosperity. Modern commercial societies were the natural home of modern liberty; because they were prosperous, they offered the chance of a rich private life to their citizens, or to those who were modestly well-off. The freedom they offered was the freedom to go our own way and enjoy ourselves in ways of our own choosing, and of course this might well include pursuing science and literature and the fine

arts. We would find life in an ancient city-state intolerable, because in such a society—Athens to some extent
excepted—everyone was always under the eye of his fellow citizens. The concept of the sanctity of private life,
which is the hallmark of modern liberalism, was entirely
unknown.

There were two morals that Constant's audience
had no difficulty in drawing. The first, directed at
Rousseau, though not by name, was that attempting to
inculcate the austere virtues of the Spartans and
Romans in modern Frenchmen was a project that could
only end in tears, or the guillotine. History is not
entirely irreversible, but modern culture has created
modern Frenchmen, and they cannot by an effort of
will turn into Spartans and Romans. Painters might
choose classical subjects to their hearts' content, but
what they were painting was modern Frenchmen in
togas. The second moral was more subtle. The modern
form of government was neither an Athenian democracy nor a Spartan oligarchy, nor—for anywhere larger
than Rousseau's Geneva—a simple republic. It had to
be a representative government, not a liberal democracy
in the modern sense of a regime with universal or near-
universal suffrage, but at all events a representative government something like the British government of the
day. That system, we should remember, gave the vote to
only around one in twelve of the adult male population.

Even after the Reform Bill of 1832, the suffrage was extended only to some one in seven adult males. But a representative system needed a wide-awake citizenry who could hold governments to account and ensure that civil liberty was respected.

That meant that the answer to the obvious question "ancient or modern liberty?" must be "both." That could not mean that we must adopt two very different worldviews, and try to adopt two opposed political, social, moral, and religious attitudes simultaneously. In essence, it was the argument that if representative government is to work properly, there must be a sufficient number of public-spirited and active citizens to fulfill their role of holding governments to account and checking their inevitable tendency to increase their own power at the expense of that of the citizen. The *point* of modern representative government was at least in large part to secure modern liberty. Nor was this only an argument for the virtues of a commercial society that was peaceable, prosperous, and, in an older idiom, "mild" in its government. Many of its virtues were, as Tocqueville was later to insist in an American context, energetic ideals of a kind to give real meaning to life. Religious liberty, for instance, was not only a matter of being free of what Hume had jauntily characterized as "the friar, the gibbet, and the stake," but a matter of being free to think and talk about deeper issues than one's daily bread. Ancient individualism certainly existed in many forms; Achilles can hardly be said to have lacked a sense of just who he was and why he was a significant being. But ancient individualism was not an individualism focused on the inner life, nor one that could imagine such a thing as self-invention in the modern sense.

But modern liberty was, self-evidently, vulnerable to several enemies. One came from the direction of such persons as Napoleon, if there could be more than one of such an astonishing figure, supposedly described by Hegel as "the spirit of the world, crowned and on horseback." The spirit of conquest was the antithesis of the commercial and mercantile spirit that writers such as Adam Smith relied on to keep the world not only safe and prosperous but in a broader sense simply rational. Persuading mankind to focus on achievable, usually but not only material, goals rather than military valor, glory, and a great name in history was one of the tasks of an Enlightenment philosophy. Tocqueville was not entirely on the side of the philosophers of "perpetual peace." Napoleonic despotism he detested, but thought the pursuit of glory a legitimate aim of a nation-state, as his enthusiasm for the French conquest of Algeria later witnessed.

The second direction from which danger might come was the revolutionary attempt to institute the republic of virtue suggested by Rousseau's admiration of Rome and Sparta and the avowed aim of Robespierre. This one might see as an excess of enthusiasm and the pursuit of a utopian vision into the last ditch. Nobody who had experienced the French Revolution wanted to rerun the experiment in 1819; Constant, somewhat improbably, had never in fact seen it at first hand, being employed at the time in a minor German princely state, but he knew very well that the sequence "monarchy, revolution, dictatorship, defeat" was not accidental. The third danger was simple lethargy. A people who had experienced the sequence of events spread over the thirty years since 1789 might very well follow Voltaire's Candide and conclude that the only sensible course of action was *cultiver son jardin*. But that posed the danger described above, that of providing no restraint on government, and failing to hold it accountable for pursuing the people's welfare.

The writer who had the most immediate impact on Tocqueville before he and Gustave de Beaumont went to America in the spring of 1831 was François Guizot. Indeed, one or two critics of the first part of *Democracy in America* complained that Tocqueville had gone to the United States with his head filled with Guizot's lectures, and had looked for confirmation in his travels of what he had expected before he went. That was an exaggeration, but it contained a grain of truth. Guizot's lectures on the history of the growth of civilization in France perhaps had a more direct influence, even if belated, on Tocqueville's *L'ancien régime* a quarter of a century after Tocqueville and Beaumont had gone to hear Guizot lecture in 1828–30. What Tocqueville took away from the two series of lectures, one an introduction to the general history of Europe from the twelfth century on and the other a parallel treatment of the development of France during the same period, was a methodological principle.

It is not altogether easy to provide a thumbnail sketch of what it was, although it is true that *Democracy in America* provides a very good example of how to do what Guizot urged, which perhaps makes an elaborate analysis unnecessary. It was the ambition to write something one might describe as "total history," examining the phenomenon whose history was at issue from every direction. History was not "the Kings and Queens of England, with some notable events," as Victorian syllabuses had it, but an attempt to describe an entire culture and its growth. Guizot also insisted that any such history must have a shape, and the driving forces that gave it that shape must be analyzed and their effects explained. The shape is provided by the movement toward social and economic, and ultimately political, equality that Tocqueville described as having the character of a divinely ordained process. Put otherwise, it is the rise of the middle class, not exactly the middle class familiar from sociological investigations of white-collar office workers in the 1950s but those whom James Mill described in 1818 as "the virtuous middle ranks" of society. Louis Hartz's *The Liberal Tradition in America* called them "petit bourgeois," although in the early years of the American Republic, they were likely to be small farmers and not an urban middle class. Crucially, they were thrifty, hardworking, eager to accumulate property and make their way in the world. They were not peasants bound to the soil under some version of a feudal order and condemned to repeat generation by generation the semiservile lives of their predecessors; a degree of social mobility was theirs for the taking.

The three countries that most obviously provided materials for reflection were Britain, France, and the United States. Guizot wrote voluminously on Britain and France. His career took him into and out of both the academy and politics, into high office and exile alike. Born in 1787, in the southern city of Nîmes, he lost his father to the guillotine in 1794 at the height of the Terror. His mother sought safety in Geneva, where Guizot must have got an excellent education; he returned to Paris in 1805, was soon very visible in literary life, became professor of history at the Sorbonne in 1812, and after the fall of Napoleon was a loyal but critical supporter of the restored Bourbon monarchy.

He held the view that a constitutional monarchy was the only possible political system for France, avoiding the absolutism of the ancien régime and Napoleon, on the one hand, and the sheer chaos of the revolutionary republic, on the other. He had a distinguished political career under Louis-Philippe, although his unaggressive policy toward Britain was not popular, and his defense of a very restricted suffrage no more so. Nonetheless, he was Louis-Philippe's longest-serving prime minister, until his career came to an abrupt end with the February Revolution of 1848. He was briefly exiled, and for the rest of his very long life devoted himself to writing history and reflecting on the political transformations of Britain and France. Although Tocqueville was his political opponent in the Chamber of Deputies during the 1840s, Guizot's ideas about the preservation of "moderate" government were among the most important influences on Tocqueville's political views, and his methodological principles were in essence Tocqueville's own.

Tocqueville was a genius. He was also quirky, rode hobbyhorses, held many views that we flinch at today, from his views on the proper place of women in American society to his much more alarming views on the legitimacy of mass murder in the interests of securing Algeria for France. He was also more elusive than he is sometimes thought to have been. Because he wrote so engagingly, the reader is often carried along with critical faculties less than fully engaged. The selections from *Democracy in America* printed here amount to only around one-tenth of that wonderful work, and have been chosen to reflect Tocqueville's continuing influence: his ideas about the inevitable march of history toward "equality of condition," his fear of the tyranny of the majority, his forebodings about the future of Native Americans, and his grim account of the impact of slavery on both the free and the slave states, his view of the essential support that religion provided to American democracy, his view of the role of American women in civilizing their menfolk, and his apprehension of a future in which "soft despotism" might be the lot of democracies that sacrificed freedom to equality. On all these, he speaks to us as our contemporary.

ON TOCQUEVILLE

Tocqueville: Democracy
and America

THE UNLIKELY AUTHOR OF
DEMOCRACY IN AMERICA

AMERICAN READERS KNOW ALEXIS de Tocqueville as the author of *Democracy in America*. French readers know him better as the author of *L'ancien régime et la révolution*. Historians of the nineteenth-century imperialist ambitions of Britain and France know him as an enthusiast for the French conquest of Algeria and a writer whose ready acceptance of the cruelties suffered by the Berbers at the hands of the French army contrasts surprisingly with his sympathy for the sufferings of Native Americans at the hands of the Anglo-Americans.[1] I begin with Tocqueville's analysis of the successes and failures of American democracy, move on to a very brief discussion of his defense of French imperialism, and end with his account of why (and when) revolutions happen, and in particular why the French Revolution made both a great deal of difference to France and almost none. First, the author himself.

It is, on the face of it, unlikely that the most significant account of American democracy should have been written by a French aristocrat, especially one who was just twenty-five years old when he began his nine-month travels through the United States in 1831–32, and only thirty when he published the first volume of *Democracy in America*. What makes it even more unlikely is that Alexis de Tocqueville came from a strongly legitimist family, who were devoted to the restored Bourbon monarchy of Louis XVIII and Charles X. He went to the United States as a result of the fall of the Bourbon monarchy in the revolution of July 1830. After the installation of the "bourgeois monarch," Louis-Philippe, the duke of Orléans, Tocqueville suffered agonies of conscience when asked to swear allegiance to the new government as a condition of continuing in his career in the national administration. Both he and his superiors thought a period of absence would reduce tensions.[2] It did not; his friend and travelling companion, Gustave de Beaumont, was suspended from his post soon after their return, and both resigned. They had both been junior magistrates at Versailles, and the purpose of the visit was to study the American penal system: *Du système pénitentiaire aux États-Unis* appeared the year after their return and was widely used as a source book on prison reform long after its authors had left the legal service. They took their ostensible reason for the journey entirely seriously. So did their American hosts, and Tocqueville complained that they tried to show him not only every prison in the country but every institution in which Americans might be involuntarily detained.

Tocqueville came from an ancient and distinguished family, whose estates were in Normandy. His parents narrowly escaped death during the Terror; one of his grandparents met his end on the scaffold, as did his great-grandfather M. de Malesherbes, the liberal-minded censor under the old regime, executed because he had defended Louis XVI at his trial. Alexis was the youngest of his father's three sons, born a decade after these terrifying events, in July 1805. Tocqueville's extended family embraced every possible attitude toward the revolution and its aftermath; distant cousins had been Jacobins, and another distant cousin adopted the children of the executed Gracchus Babeuf; some served Napoleon, as others later served Louis-Philippe and Louis Bonaparte. Tocqueville's father, Hervé, was a constitutionally minded aristocrat of the kind his son discussed in *L'ancien régime*; events turned him into a monarchist and legitimist, happy to serve the heirs of

Louis XVI and unwilling to serve anyone else. He rose to be *préfet* of several departments, including finally Seine-et-Oise, the summit of prefectorial ambitions. Its headquarters were in Versailles, where Hervé enjoyed the life of a courtier-administrator. His public life came to an end with the July Revolution, in 1830. He retired, and lived till 1856, dying at the age of eighty-four, only three years before Alexis.

Brought up in a pious, conservative household, in a family for whom public service at the highest level was both a duty and a right, Tocqueville was confided to the care of the abbé Leseur, who had been tutor to his father and his two older brothers, Hippolyte and Édouard. The abbé was a religious conservative and energetically contemptuous of liberals and liberalism, but a benign and encouraging tutor who took pains to develop his pupil's intellect. The teenage Tocqueville had a distinguished academic career at the lycée in Metz, went on to study law in Paris, and graduated in 1826. He joined the government legal service as a second best to the military career he was not healthy enough to contemplate. His writings reflect his sense of what he had missed when they praise both the humdrum, everyday, cheerful prosperity that the Americans achieved as rational law-abiding creatures and the glory that the French might achieve through their imperial exploits in Algeria.

In 1827 he was appointed *juge auditeur*. Before he

could become bored with life as a bureaucrat, the revolution of 1830 put an end to the Bourbon monarchy and installed Louis-Philippe. Tocqueville gritted his teeth and swore allegiance, alienating his most fiercely legitimist relatives in the process. Soon afterward he and his friend and colleague Gustave de Beaumont devised their plan to visit the United States to examine its penal system. Since they would go at their own expense, their superiors saw no reason to refuse their request for leave, even though they kept them waiting six months for permission. On May 9, 1831, they arrived in New York.

Democracy in America has held an honored place in the canon of political analysis for almost two centuries. Its author wanted literary fame rather than an afterlife in political science syllabuses, and a career at the summit of French politics. *Democracy* was written for the audience that had the first in its gift, and he hoped literary fame would launch him on the path to the second. The publication of the first volume of *Democracy*, in 1835, made him famous; the publication of the second volume, in 1840, led to his election to the Académie Française a year later. Fame liberated him in other ways. Throughout his youth he had fallen in love with unsuitable women—unsuitable as a matter of social standing. At the age of thirty, with a position in the world, and his mother dead, he could do as he chose, and he married Mary Mottley, a very ordinary middle-class Englishwoman whose exact age was uncertain, but who was at least six years older than he. It was an oddly successful marriage, though far from easy. They were ill-assorted, but devoted. She became a devout Catholic; he lost his faith in his teens and never got it back. He became a somewhat dilute deist, interested in mysticism, unhappy that he could not confide in his wife, and aware of the jealousy she felt for his confidante in these matters, Mme Swetchine.[3]

Tocqueville's ultimate ambitions were political; in 1837 he failed to be elected to the National Assembly, but succeeded two years after. He was a significant but not a successful figure; he was too visibly contemptuous of the bourgeois politicians whom he had to cultivate for success. In any case, he was opposed to the ministries of the 1840s and seemed destined to permanent opposition. The upheavals that began with the revolution of February 1848 that evicted Louis-Philippe and ended with Louis Bonaparte's coup d'état of December 1851 did not show him at his best. He mocked his sister-in-law for panicking in the face of the revolution, but came close to panic himself. This was intellectual, not physical, panic. His coolness in the face of physical danger was impressive; but his incomprehension of the causes of the revolution was surprising, and his reaction to the misery of the poor ungenerous. Nonetheless, his memoirs of the revolution are engrossing.[4] The underlying cause of the discontent that toppled Louis-Philippe was economic: a string of bad harvests brought ruin and near-famine to the countryside and raised the price of necessities in the cities. The way to preserve political stability was to relieve economic distress by any means possible. Mistakes would be corrigible once there was a decent harvest, social peace, and revived economic activity. Tocqueville's economics was that of the conservative wing of the Manchester school, and he saw measures of relief as steps toward expropriation and the guillotine. Like the British in the face of famine in Ireland, the interim government installed by the revolution responded to falling revenues with retrenchment, exacerbating the problem. When the Parisian workers rose in revolt in June 1848, Tocqueville's allies shot them down.

Things did not turn out as he expected. General Cavaignac, who had suppressed the uprising during the June Days, was defeated in the presidential elections of December 1848 by Louis Bonaparte. Tocqueville detested Bonaparte, but accepted the post of foreign minister in the Barrot government of 1849; when the government fell, he lost office and made it clear that he did not wish to serve again. He remained a member of the National Assembly, and served on the committee appointed to devise a new constitution for the Second Republic; his fame as an expert on the American Constitution gave him credibility, but his enthusiasm for American institutions alienated his fellow members. His political life came to an end with Louis Bonaparte's coup d'état of December 1851; it is possible that Tocqueville's one success in promoting American ideas about constitutions provoked the event: he persuaded the assembly to put term limits on the presidency. Faced with enforced retirement, Bonaparte took the obvious next step. Tocqueville was already very ill with tuberculosis, and until his death, in 1859, he led the life of a retired scholar. During his last years, he wrote the first part of a long-projected history of the French Revolution, *L'ancien régime et la révolution*. When John Stuart Mill wrote to thank Tocqueville for the gift of a copy of the book, he observed that few men had written three distinct masterpieces: the two volumes of *Democracy*, so different from one another, and *L'ancien régime*. Mill's praise was not excessive.[5] One modern critic thinks *Souvenirs*, his account of the 1848 revolution, is even better.[6]

DEMOCRACY IN AMERICA AND DEMOCRACY IN AMERICA: MOTIVATION

Tocqueville's ideas have been exploited by left and right; modern conservatives praise his strictures on big government and his enthusiasm for decentralization, many American liberals praise his concern with association and community, and everyone praises his devotion to political liberty. American politicians bask in his praise of their political system and overlook his contempt for the "coarse appearance" of the members of the House of Representatives.[7] Few readers notice his enthusiasm for the brutal methods of punishment he found in American prisons, and not many notice the repressiveness of his views on family life.

Tocqueville is elusive, but not unplaceable. French interest in the United States sprang from the French failure to bring the revolution of 1789 to a successful conclusion. French assistance to the rebellious colonies after 1776 had nothing to do with an enthusiasm for republican government, but was part of a French strategy to recover the ground the country had lost to Britain during the Seven Years' War—the war that ended with the British seizure of French India and much of French North America. Americans saw their revolution as the inspiration for an age of political renovation: free republics would everywhere replace hereditary monarchies and aristocracies. This was not the purpose to which Louis XVI's government committed its navy and seconded army commanders. The leaders of the American Revolution were not deceived; they understood that Spain and France helped them evict the British to protect their position to the south, west, and northwest of the thirteen liberated colonies, and they were unapologetic about making a quick and separate peace with the

British to avert future trouble with their allies. None-theless, a liberal-minded Frenchman would feel a degree of paternal pride in the United States, and a patriotic Frenchman would see the United States as an ally in cutting Britain down to size.

America posed a deeply interesting question to any Frenchman with the political curiosity to ask it. How had Americans launched a revolution that aimed at establishing a free, stable, and constitutional govern-ment and made a success of it, while the French had in forty-one years lurched from absolute monarchy to con-stitutional monarchy, to the declaration of the republic, to mob rule, the Terror and mass murder, and thence to a conservative republic, Napoleonic autocracy, the Bourbon restoration, further revolution, and the instal-lation of an Orleanist constitutional monarchy? Up to a point, the answer was obvious; the Americans claimed—not wholly plausibly—that they were reluctant revolu-tionaries; they wanted to regain the English liberties they had exercised until the tyrannical Parliament of George III and his ministers tried to destroy them. Self-government was a long-established reality in colonial America; the collapse of British rule was followed not by anarchy but by the citizens governing themselves much as before. The democratization of institutions during the American Revolution was to some extent rolled back afterward; but independence was not a leap into the unknown. It was more nearly a leap into the past of the English Civil War, when the New Model Army learned to govern itself and the country by committees answerable to the rank and file. If Washington had been Cromwell, the American Revolution might have ended in military dictatorship; but if Washington had been Cromwell, he would not have been accepted as commander in chief of the Continental army.

That history raised the question of what the social and political attitudes were that meant that in one society individuals could cooperate and make self-government possible, while in another they could not, why the inhabitants of one country were active and ambitious and able to pursue "self-interest rightly understood," and those of another country were not. A stable political order that was both democratic and liberal required distinctive social, moral, and economic attachments; their analysis was an urgent task. These attachments constituted what social scientists later called "political culture," and what Montesquieu had studied as *les moeurs*; they were the product of the distinctive geographical setting of the American experiment and a colonial history of some duration. The United States came into existence as an independent nation-state almost two centuries after the first British colonists had arrived; many things, from the open frontier to the absence of feudalism, to the religious allegiances of the first colonists, shaped the attitudes and created the abilities that allowed Americans to make their revolution without descending into anarchy.

The new republic then reinforced the culture that reinforced it. There was a virtuous circle: the political system gave the citizens an intense attachment to the political system; their attachment helped it to function effectively, and its effectiveness made the citizens still more attached to it. Equally interesting were the indirect supports that enabled the political system to combine popular sovereignty and individual liberty. Tocqueville was particularly impressed by the role of women; although they had almost complete freedom as girls, they became the guardians of respectability once they were married. They exercised a psychological and moral discipline that was badly needed in a raw new country. The benign moral tutelage exerted by American women ensured that enough men were sufficiently public-spirited and law-abiding to govern themselves without anarchy, and that in a highly decentralized country communities could be efficiently self-policing.[8]

TOCQUEVILLE'S INFLUENCES: ROUSSEAU, MONTESQUIEU, GUIZOT

Tocqueville was sometimes criticized for having gone to America full of preconceptions. "He had thought too much before he had seen anything" was one comment. Whether or not he had thought *too* much before he looked, he certainly went with a mind well stocked with ideas about the prospects of popular government in the nineteenth century. One source was Rousseau, one of the two thinkers whom Tocqueville said he thought about every day. This is surprising because Rousseau was a philosopher; he was also a composer, a novelist, and a speculative historian, but he was the philosopher who inspired Kant's moral and political philosophy. Tocqueville was not a philosopher, but a political sociologist, even though he had strong opinions about the meaning of human existence. Rousseau analyzed natural right, individual interest, and the common good, in ways that Kant and later writers took up and extended, and academic philosophers still do; Tocqueville did not. Tocqueville had the sensibilities of a sociologist and a historian and the political intuitions of a statesman; he thought the spectacle of American democracy astonishing and wished to know whence it had sprung, how it worked, and what its prospects were. Rousseau's inquest into the legitimacy of the state and his location of that legitimacy in the moral authority of the general will were not Tocqueville's concerns.

Rousseau's impact is nonetheless easily explained. Not only America but the whole Western world were imbued with the spirit of equality that Rousseau had articulated in the *Social Contract* and *Discourse on the Origin of Inequality*. What equality entailed in social, economic, and political contexts was disputable; the compatibility of equality in one realm with equality in another was uncertain; it was also essential to discover what kinds of equality sustained liberty and what kinds of equality threatened it. *Democracy* and *L'ancien régime* were eloquent on these points. The new belief in human equality was part of the rise of individualism. Rousseau was as eloquent as Tocqueville on good and bad forms of individuality; Tocqueville was not at odds with Rousseau on this topic. Bad individualism—which Tocqueville tended to call "individualism" without qualification—was a form of self-centeredness quite different from a strong sense of ourselves as moral beings with duties to perform and rights to protect. That was good individualism or individuality. Bad individualism was driven by fear; and its psychological impact on political life was potentially disastrous. Its conception of equality would inspire us to drag others down to our own level rather than inspiring us to cooperate with them to elevate the moral and intellectual level of us all. The egalitarianism that feared all difference and resented all superiority was inimical to variety and change. It was from Tocqueville's plangent discussion in the second volume of *Democracy* that Mill learned the fear that animates *On Liberty*. Although equality and sameness are logically distinct, a democratic—more exactly a "mass"—society would confound them.[9] Nonetheless, in the right conditions, emphasized in the first part of *Democracy*, equality of condition promoted liberty, by promoting self-reliance and ambition. Rousseau's emphasis on the moral equality that a rights-respecting regime is committed to was not alien to Tocqueville, even if he was not disposed to rehearse issues in moral philosophy.

Montesquieu had raised many of the same anxieties as Rousseau about the incompatibility of classical ideals of political virtue and classical standards of patriotic self-sacrifice with the comfortable, commercial, self-interested values of the modern world. His style was closer to Tocqueville's own; he was a sociologically minded political analyst, less inclined than Rousseau to complain about the world he was analyzing. He wanted to understand the impact of climate and geography and domestic life and what we have for a century called "political socialization"—the process of bringing up children to understand the political arrangements of their society and induce a sufficient loyalty to them (or perhaps a sufficient loyalty to other features of our society to induce a thoroughgoing disgust with the political arrangements under which they live).

Montesquieu was thoroughly, and rightly, frightened of both the despotism of one man and the damage that religious and ideological passion could do. This prompted him to explain the virtues of French absolute monarchy and its difference from Ottoman despotism in terms of its "moderation." Unlike despotism, it was not a regime of fear. Individuals owned their own property as something other than the revocable gift of their ruler; French subjects were not the slaves of their sovereign; they might not be Spartan citizens, let alone Athenians, but they were not Persian slaves. Like any regime that depended on a balance of forces, French monarchy was vulnerable to pressures that might render it much less defensible; this was why *les moeurs* were so important. The extrapolitical attitudes, allegiances, habits, and beliefs that maintained a consensus on what was and was not tolerable within the existing political order provided the shock-absorbing mechanisms that allowed the political system to operate, and to secure the attachment of the French people to the regime.

Tocqueville spent his life as an intellectual brooding—as volume 2 of *Democracy* and *L'ancien régime* attest—on the strengths and weaknesses of the prerevolutionary monarchy and on the nature of despotism. It was not only his eighteenth-century predecessors whom he listened to. Before he went to the United States, he spent two years listening to François Guizot's lectures called "The History of Civilization in Europe." The critics who said that Tocqueville had thought too much before he saw the United States meant that he went imbued with Guizot's vision of the causes of social change, and with many of Guizot's political attachments; the first was true, the second not. The British had become the most successful modern nation because they had absorbed the rising middle class into a stable political system; the English constitutional monarchy had diverted into useful channels the populist energies that exploded in the French Revolution because they had not been made use of earlier. The "principle of antagonism," and especially the need to maintain and find room for the expression of an antagonism of opinions in order to sustain an open, lively, and progressive society had been usefully embodied in English institutions. The moral was that democracy—in a loose and unpolitical sense that embraced an egalitarian social climate and social and economic mobility rather than universal suffrage and institutions to give effect to the popular will—was irresistible, but had to be directed by a wise political elite. When Tocqueville said in *Democracy* that a new political science was required for a new world, he was agreeing with Guizot.

In their politics, narrowly speaking, Tocqueville and Guizot were not at one. Guizot was a willing Orleanist and Tocqueville not; Guizot saw his political role as that of a barrier to the left, and before 1848 Tocqueville thought safety lay in giving the left a larger role in French politics. As foreign minister and prime minister,

Guizot promoted a foreign policy that would conciliate the British and avoid the diversion of French energies into the pursuit of ephemeral glory, while Tocqueville was a less cautious imperialist and colonialist. Guizot's influence was on Tocqueville's analytical approach, and on his preconceptions about what he would find in America, the country that, as Mill said after reading both Guizot and Tocqueville, epitomized the rise of an essentially provincial middle class.[10]

THE FRENCHNESS OF
DEMOCRACY IN AMERICA

Rousseau, Montesquieu, and Guizot gave Tocqueville his intellectual bearings and taught him how to frame his questions. America gave him his inspiration, but it was France that he thought about. *Democracy in America* is a book about America; but it is also a very French book about France. It could not have been written by an Englishman or even by an American. This is not only because English visitors who went to the United States wrote snobbish little books about the appalling table manners of the American middle classes; the French did that as well, and Tocqueville's reactions to his hosts' manners were equally sharp; but he knew it did not matter, and he left his observations in his private letters. No English writer could have begun volume 2 of *Democracy* as Tocqueville did, by observing that the Americans are an unphilosophical people, among whom the ideas of Descartes can make no headway, but who nonetheless behave as practical Cartesians: "America is thus one of the countries of the world where the precepts of Descartes are least studied and most widely applied. We need not be surprised by that."[11]

The genius of Americans for starting from scratch and inventing what they needed was a commonplace; the usual and wholly plausible view was that it was born of the fact that they were building a new civilization in the wilderness. It took a Frenchman to draw a philosophical moral and describe it as practical Cartesianism; it may well have taken a Frenchman who had lost his own Catholic faith, but who thought that religion was a vital ingredient in *les moeurs* that sustained American democracy. Analyzing the idea of America was not unintelligible to English observers in the 1830s; if it had been, they could not have read Tocqueville as they did. Nonetheless, the contrasts Tocqueville had in mind were overwhelmingly between American attitudes and beliefs and those of his countrymen; when he says "we," as he often does, it is "we French." English readers found him puzzling, and even Mill admitted that his writing was "abstruse" and suffered from a lack of illustrations to enable his readers to see what he meant. The greater difficulty was that he was drawing contrasts between the mores of Americans and the mores of Frenchmen for French readers.

There are simpler ways in which *Democracy* is very French. Where Tocqueville has a chance to praise the French temperament and dispraise the Anglo-Saxon, he takes it. The nationalist politician of the later 1830s and 1840s was present on his younger self's American journey. The suggestion that Tocqueville went to the United States to see France more clearly might be thought fanciful; but we reach the same point if we begin entirely unfancifully. The Americans had created a republic, and, as Benjamin Franklin had said at the time, the question was whether they could keep it. They had. One did not have to believe that they had created utopia to believe that they had done something astonishing; moreover, they had done what the French could not. The British were not relevant; on one view of British history, the British had rightly not tried again to create another republic after making such a bad job of it in 1649; on another, they had reduced the monarch to a hereditary president for life and dressed up a de facto parliamentary republic in the costume of a de jure constitutional monarchy. Tocqueville could not know that he would live to see the short-lived Second Republic and the early years of the Second Empire, but he knew that in America he must discover what was possible in France.

Tocqueville was not a republican. He thought France would be better off with a constitutional monarchy; but he knew history was not on his side. Montesquieu's recipe for a moderate modern monarchy required a social order in which political power rested in the hands of intermediate social groups; it needed not a small and exclusive nobility but a large and permeable gentry and a self-confident and responsible bourgeoisie. The lesson was drawn from England, but made sense of America. Tocqueville's view, expressed in *L'ancien régime* but already in place in *Democracy*, was that Louis XIV and his successors had undermined their own position by hollowing out the social hierarchy. The French nobility was bribed with financial privileges to accept the loss of political power; as a result there was no shock absorber between the monarchy and the populace. This analysis rested on a familiar view of the connection between political legitimacy and social function. Deference to our superiors comes easily when they are doing something useful; if they bear more than their share of military service, staff the local system of justice, and represent the district in parliament, we may think they are richer and more privileged than they absolutely deserve, but not that they are parasites. Functionless privilege can only rest on sullen acquiescence or fear.

So Tocqueville looked at America and saw France, talked to Americans and thought of his fellow Frenchmen. *Democracy in America* is an insightful account of the egalitarian United States of 1831, and an eerily prescient analysis of liberal democracy almost two centuries later, written for a French audience. Thanks to John Stuart Mill as much as anyone, it came to be understood as a tract on what was later called "mass society" and a book *for* Americans as well as about them; it also came to be understood as a tract for the English. *On Liberty* would have been a different book, and perhaps not written at all, if Mill had not read *Democracy in America,* and more especially the second volume with its reflections on the quiet despotism to which a mass society might succumb.

EQUALITY AS A PROVIDENTIAL FORCE

If *Democracy* generated morals that Tocqueville expected his readers to find universally applicable, the reason was that what was unmissable in America was becoming visible in Europe. Tocqueville's central claim was that increasing social equality was an unstoppable force transforming Western society. How long this had been happening was less clear; sometimes Tocqueville suggested that what was visible in nineteenth-century Europe was the culmination of processes at work since the eleventh century, and sometimes he relied on the

more familiar contrast between inegalitarian, aristocratic societies and their egalitarian bourgeois successors that suggested that recent changes mattered more.[12]
The claim that there was an irresistible movement
toward the "equalization of conditions" underpinned
one of Tocqueville's methodological claims. He said
that the new world required a new political science for
its analysis, but did not say whether he thought he had
devised it or what it was.

Tocqueville's comments on equality sometimes
sound more providential than scientific. The implacable
progress of equality, described as a river that may be
channeled but cannot be stopped in its course, suggests
to Tocqueville that the process is of divine origin; it is
not only the outcome of one thing after another, economic change, intellectual change, moral change, and so
on.[13] His readiness to see the hand of God in the process
was not just a figure of speech; Tocqueville emphasized
the contrast between the viewpoint of the human
observer forced to look at a small slice of the historical
process and extrapolate as best he can, and that of God,
who grasps the whole process in one intellectual moment,
needing no generalizations or extrapolations. There is
little point in speculating about how far Tocqueville
might have pressed the point, since he eschewed methodological commentary on his own work. Mill gave a
down-to-earth account of Tocqueville's achievement.

Tocqueville had demonstrated the method of a true social science; he had founded his insights into political change upon both a knowledge of fundamental human nature and a knowledge of historical trends. Tocqueville was happy to be praised as a genius but not explicit about how far he accepted Mill's account of what his genius consisted in.

DEMOCRACY IN AMERICA: VOLUME 1 VERSUS VOLUME 2

The two volumes of *Democracy* are very different in tone, the first strikingly optimistic about the prospects for the United States and democracy, the second much more uncertain; they are also laid out very differently. The change of approach and expectations between the two volumes is more than enough to justify Mill's observation that they were two masterpieces rather than two halves of one masterpiece. The first volume is not unphilosophical or unreflective, but it hews closer than the second to the task of giving an account of how the United States came into existence, what its salient features are, politically, socially, and intellectually, how relations are conducted between the various social classes—Tocqueville was one of the first visitors to be struck by the way in which almost all issues in the

United States were turned into legal issues—and how the religious and moral outlook of Americans sustains their "experiment in liberty."

The first volume was far more than a report to his countrymen by a very clever young man who had taken a close look at the United States; but Tocqueville's introduction suggests that it is at least that. The organization of the book—eighteen chapters in two sections, each chapter broken into very short discussions of particular points—matches the briskness of the style. The first eight chapters introduce the country, its history and its Constitution, and the next ten show the political system in operation. The first volume is firmly focused on democratic political institutions and on the federal system within which the Americans had embedded them. There is a great deal of commentary on the social, economic, and moral conditions that enabled the Americans to make such a success of democracy; the final chapter contains Tocqueville's famously anxious discussion under the title "The Present State and Probable Future of the Three Races That Inhabit America"; but the book is essentially an answer to the question of how the Americans maintain with such success a stable but lively democracy.

The second volume, in contrast, is organized as four distinct sections, focused on the intellectual life of the United States, on the "sentiments" of the Amer-

ican people, on the "morals"—essentially *les moeurs*—
of a democracy, and finally on how they come together
in affecting the political outlook of Americans. Quite
apart from the more pessimistic tone of the whole volume, there is a change of focus from the success of a
lively, if chaotic, political system to the cultural fail-
ings of mass society. The explanation of the change
did not owe much to Tocqueville's reassessment of the
American evidence; the nine months he spent there
were all he saw of America at first hand, though he
kept up a correspondence with the friends he had made
for the rest of his life.[14] French political life cast a
shadow over his memory of America. The question to
which the first volume had offered an optimistic answer
was whether equality and liberty are compatible with
each other, and the answer was that in the United
States they are. The natural conclusion, and the burden of Tocqueville's argument, is that *les moeurs* are
favorable to liberty in the United States and that in
France they are not. The political culture of the United
States had not changed dramatically, but Tocqueville
had thought further about the less attractive aspects of
Jacksonian America, and his characteristic melancholy
reasserted itself when the vivacity of everyday American life had faded from memory and French political
life was a daily irritant.

DEMOCRACY ONE

Tocqueville began by saying that a wholly new world needs a new political science to interpret it. What he provided was what Max Weber later described as an "ideal type" analysis. He wanted to reveal the essence of democracy by heightening some empirical phenomena and neglecting others, in order to achieve a sharper picture of the forces sweeping modern societies toward a more egalitarian future. The reader who looks for definitions of Tocqueville's key terms looks in vain; we get a portrait of America, not a photograph. Better, it is a film rather than a photograph: there is a narrative of the movement that generated democracy; it is a narrative of increasing equality of "conditions." *Equality of condition* is the crucial phenomenon under discussion—what creates it, and what its political consequences are. When Mill reviewed volume I of *Democracy*, he complained mildly that Tocqueville talked of democracy—which is essentially a political notion and means, as it says, the rule of the people—but wrote about equality. Mill wished to distinguish sharply between the radical demand for universal suffrage on the one hand and social and economic equality on the other. When he wrote *On Liberty*, he himself conflated the two, much as Tocqueville had done.

Equality of condition was not equality of income, education, or anything in particular; it consisted in the absence of social obstacles to whatever ambitions an American entertained. Critics complain that Tocqueville underestimated the extent of economic inequality in the United States, which may well be true; but he was looking at the contrast between his own country and the United States, and was struck by what observers are still struck by—that almost all Americans believed they belonged to the middle class. Some 90 percent of Americans in the early twenty-first century report themselves as "middle class," with more than 50 percent declaring themselves as "middle middle class."

The first volume of *Democracy* is a long argument with historical illustrations. The argument is that in the United States *the people* truly rule, and that there—perhaps there alone—they rule without the danger of a relapse into anarchy or tyranny. Not everything in the United States is admirable; but their example poses to the French the question why the Americans can do what "we" cannot. So we can pursue Tocqueville along the two tracks of his argument: first, that the American people truly rule, nontyrannically, nonchaotically, and preserving the civil liberties of all save slaves and Native Americans, and, second, what enables them to do it.

That the people truly rule is the theme of one of Tocqueville's characteristically brief chapters; it opens part 2 of the first volume and recites the obvious fact that in the United States almost every position of authority is not only elective but requires reelection every year or two; not only legislators but judges in most jurisdictions, and the executive everywhere, answer almost continuously to the people. The surprisingness of this to a Frenchmen used to a hereditary king, senators for life, a very restricted electorate, and a judiciary that was part of the royal bureaucracy can hardly be exaggerated. Tocqueville immediately observes that when we talk of the people governing, we must recall that "it is the majority that governs in the name of the people," bringing to the fore the question raised by Madison and Jefferson of the conditions under which the rule of the people degenerates into the tyranny of the majority. Here he deflates the anxiety by observing that the majority consists for the most part of peaceful citizens who sincerely desire the good of their country, but the anxiety is only momentarily set on one side. Although the majority is composed of peaceful citizens wanting the good of their country, the majority is omnipotent, and defenses against it nonexistent.[15]

Tocqueville's discussion of the tyranny of the majority rests on more than one thought. He assumes that sovereignty, in the Hobbesian sense, must reside somewhere. Like many political philosophers, he thought that in every political and legal system there must somewhere be an absolute and unconstrained power. Critics of the Hobbesian view, a view held not only by Bentham and his followers but by Blackstone as well, point to the United States as a legal and political system where there is no Hobbesian sovereign; it is one system, but does not receive its unity from a sovereign. Tocqueville ignores this line of reasoning. The majority is the sovereign, and absolute; and because there is no appeal against the majority, it is strictly speaking despotic. This is not an absurd thought. Mill held that the government of India by the East India Company was a despotism. It was a benign despotism; and the company was itself regulated by the British government. Nonetheless, it was not answerable to its Indian subjects and was therefore a despotism.

The majority in a democracy is not answerable to the minority, and is strictly in the position of any other despot; but the argument claims too much. It is a logical truth that in all regimes there must be a point at which appeals against legal and political decisions or legislation come to an end, and the losers must either acquiesce or take up arms. It is not a truth at all that any person or group has despotic authority. The U.S. Constitution puts innumerable obstacles in the way of anyone trying to exercise tyrannical power; the president cannot dissolve Congress, but must wait for elections to provide him with a more compliant Congress, if he is lucky. Congress cannot remove the president in the way the English Parliament can remove ministers and governments. Long before Tocqueville went to the United States, the Supreme Court had acquired for itself the authority to declare legislation unconstitutional, even if passed by Congress and signed by the president. If an enraged majority wants to do something that is at present unconstitutional, and presses for changes in the Constitution, it must endure whatever delays it takes for Congress and the individual states to pass the amendment by a sufficient majority. It can be done; during World War I, the Eighteenth Amendment to the Constitution was passed over the veto of President Wilson, and ratified in 1919. It prohibited the sale of alcoholic beverages and had mixed results; it saved many Americans from alcohol-related diseases and opened up a profitable trade for gangsters and bootleggers; and it was repealed by the Twenty-First Amendment in 1933. Whether the fact that it took three years to pass into law and less than one to repeal is a sad commentary on human nature, or a reassuring one, is not at issue. The point is that it takes a long and sustained campaign to pass a constitutional amendment, which makes it very difficult for an enraged majority to rewrite the fundamental rules to suit itself.

Tocqueville knew this. The first part of volume I of *Democracy* gives a long account of the history and geography of the country and its constitutional arrangements. Like other observers, he pointed out that America was to an extraordinary degree a country ruled by lawyers. He thought this was one of its virtues, which may have owed something to pride in his own profession. However that may be, he understood that the constitutional arrangements of the United States were intended to do two things at once, to establish an effective national government and to prevent any faction, even what Madison called the "majority faction," from exercising untrammeled power. He also understood the effects of the way the Constitution gave large and small states identical representation in the Senate, and how it was part of the effort to take the issue of slavery off the agenda. In thinking about Tocqueville's anxieties about the tyranny of the majority, we should recall that the barriers to majority tyranny protected slave owners more effectively than religious minorities and eccentrics.

It is puzzling that Tocqueville supposed that the majority was omnipotent; to an English observer, familiar with the sovereignty of Parliament, it seemed then, as now, that majorities faced innumerable obstacles in getting their own way, and that the most impressive feature of American politics is the ability of well-placed interest groups to extract benefits from the political system that the majority cannot. But like Madison, Tocqueville thought that laws were "parchment barriers." The omnipotence of the majority was a deep fact about American life, and ran deeper than the Constitution. To understand how deep, we must briefly explore Tocqueville's explanation of why the English succeeded in settling America and the French did not. The paradox is that the French did everything needed for success and failed, while the English gave hardly a thought to the matter and succeeded. That had immense consequences for the way Americans—Anglo-Americans—thought of themselves. The French government intended there to be properly organized colonies up and down the Mississippi valley, took pains to understand the geography, climate, soil, and anything else about which information could be had, and placed military settlements in sensible places; it supplied them with efficient government on the French model. They did not thrive; they did not grow, but shrank. When the British found them an obstacle, they brushed them aside.

Conversely, the eastern shores of America were settled by Englishmen who as often as not were fleeing their home government or their creditors. Although the British government claimed sovereignty over their affairs and sent out royal governors, the governments of the colonies were contrived by the emigrants on a self-help basis. Some colonists disliked the governments they had set up as much as they disliked the one they had escaped, and set off to find somewhere where they could establish a community more to their liking. These unorganized and spontaneous communities thrived. It does not follow that Englishmen and Frenchmen are members of wholly different races, although Tocqueville sometimes suggests they might be. Tocqueville's account of the different behavior of the French and English governments of the seventeenth and eighteenth centuries is the key to the underlying claim. French governmental tutelage could do much, but it enervated the individual Frenchman; English neglect liberated the energies of the colonists. That greatly affected *les moeurs* of Anglo-Americans.

There are many problems in Tocqueville's account of his fellow countrymen. He sometimes suggests that the French were essentially stay-at-homes, and sometimes the opposite: the French sought glory while the English did not. To add a final complexity he also observed, as others had, that the English were rarely tempted to slip out of white society and turn themselves into Native Americans. They did not intermarry with Native Americans, and English trappers and hunters did not merge with the other inhabitants of the wilderness, as their French counterparts did. It is initially difficult to discern what Tocqueville is up to. It is very hard to see the pursuit of glory, the search for domestic tranquility, and a happy return to the life of the noble savage as the major influences on a group of people; the different passions seem too much at odds with one another.

One can rescue Tocqueville, and when we see how, we have the clue to the tyranny of the majority. Tocqueville asks why the English ended up settling America and colonizing the country in ways the French could not. The shortest answer would be "Puritanism," not so much Calvinist Protestantism as the mind-set invoked by Max Weber in *The Protestant Ethic and the Spirit of Capitalism*. Compared with the French in their stay-at-home moods, the Englishman will not live under a government to which he has not consented, and will not accept the boundaries of his present world as those he must accept. Compared with the Frenchman in search of glory, the Englishman will stick patiently to the task he has set himself and beat the wilderness into fertile farmland and pasture. Unlike the Frenchman ready to succumb to the charms of the wilderness, he thinks the wilderness is to be tamed and made useful. His character has drawbacks; it can be hard, narrow, and unimaginative. It is unthinking about the losses suffered by those who get in the way: Native Americans, black slaves, and the perceivedly idle and ignorant of all races.

The United States exists because Englishmen of this kind created the new republic. Imbued with a strong sense of their own rectitude, they set up political institutions that amplified the authority of the majority. Tocqueville knew that the common European view of America was that the government was feeble; observers envied the freedom of American citizens, but were struck by how little authority the federal government wielded and how few levers of power were at its disposal. Tocqueville turns the thought around. What is impressive is not how much freedom Americans possess but how little. He was impressed by how little protection they had against its loss and how far the political system reinforced the authority of the majority. A nontyrannical government requires the possibility of an appeal from the decisions of one authority to another authority that can exercise a check. In America, says Tocqueville, no such check exists. The reason is the omnipresence and omnipotence of public opinion. Every institution is an instrument of public opinion; the legislature reflects public opinion, so the laws it passes reflect public opinion; judges are elected by the people and hold their posts only so long as they implement the law in ways that reflect public opinion. To say that the majority is omnipotent is to say that public opinion is omnipresent and omnipotent. The institutional checks and balances that a legalistic view of the American Constitution emphasizes impressed him less than the ability of public opinion to bypass them.

Nonetheless, America remains free because in practical matters Americans are self-reliant, uninclined to exert their power over one another to the limits of what is possible, and able to organize their lives with little assistance from, or control by, government. Tocqueville writes wryly about the contrast between France and America as regards the invisibility of central government; Americans respond to the absence of the tutelage that the French state aspires to provide by organizing themselves to provide what they need for themselves. Everything hangs together: tasks like jury service force Americans to play a part in public affairs and provide a form of political education. Vast numbers of local newspapers reinforce this political education, and their varied allegiances ensure that the uniformity of opinion to which democracy is vulnerable is constantly broken up and has to reform against opposition.

Tocqueville's recipe for the survival of liberty within a democratic society is not *only* a matter of preserving the "antagonism of opinions," but that antagonism is vital. It does not rest on nothing, as though American society was a debating society. Tocqueville acknowledges the foundations of political debate in economic life. America was the paradigmatic land of opportunity. He was writing before the great period of westward expansion, and before the trading and industrial cities of the east coast and the Mississippi took in Catholic migrants from southern and central Europe, Jews from eastern Europe, radical German and Austro-Hungarian exiles after 1848, and so on. Still, by European standards, the thrust westward was already astonishing.

The American economy was agricultural—in the broad sense that included the tobacco, cotton, and sugar produced for distant markets by slave labor—and mercantile, with cities springing up in the interior to service small-scale industry and the processing of agricultural products. The textile industry of New England was growing fast, but the industrialization built on Pennsylvania coal and iron was still thirty years away. America was nonetheless much more prosperous than European societies at the same level of development; the emigrant looked around him and contrasted his situation in America with his situation in Europe, and was content.

Different regions had different interests, saw the world differently; this diversity of economic interests kept political debate bubbling. It nonetheless stayed within bounds. American religion in particular kept American citizens self-disciplined, respectable; it was also important in making them take worldly success seriously as a badge of respectability. Tocqueville's interest in religion was implicit in his Montesequieuan assumptions: physical causes made a difference to the success of a nontyrannical republic, since some climates fostered despotism and others self-reliance, and bred citizens who would not brook tyranny; the laws made much more difference; and *les moeurs* made the greatest difference. Religion, both in the sense of belief and more importantly in the sense of social practice, was a central part of *les moeurs*. The Americans had contrived a surprising device for making religion a powerful social force. They had written the complete separation of church and state into the Constitution. Unlike ancien régime France, America had no alliance of wealthy and useless clergy with wealthy and useless aristocrats. Whatever reasons Americans might have for disliking their government could not turn into anti-clericalism; conversely, if they were disaffected from whatever church they belonged to, they could move to another or set one up from scratch. The prerevolutionary French union of church and state implicated each in the unpopularity of the other. It was a familiar observation that anticlericalism is more common in Catholic countries than in Protestant ones; Tocqueville was less interested in that fact than in the prospects for the survival of religion in a bustling, progressive, and modernizing society. He thought American democracy needed the support of religion more than more traditional and hierarchical societies. The restlessness of an egalitarian people and the economic uncertainty—for both the prosperous and the less successful—that permeated such a society demanded an antidote. Religion created the "habits of the heart" that provided consolation in the midst of misfortune and steadiness in the midst of uncertainty.

Tocqueville ends the first volume of *Democracy* with

some somber reflections on the relations between "the three races" that coexist in the United States. They are the white Europeans, the American Indians, and the Negro slaves. Tocqueville had no doubt that the Indians were doomed and that their extinction was a moral disaster. The bleakness of this assessment was characteristic of Tocqueville; he had a strong sense of the difference between what was inevitable and what was admirable. The extinction of the Native Americans is a moral disaster not only because the cruelty with which they are treated is disgusting, nor only because the white government has violated every treaty it has signed, and respects its own agreements merely as long as it is convenient—though these are actions of which any decent person should be ashamed. It is also a disaster because it is the destruction of an essentially aristocratic way of life. Set against the humdrum, self-centered placidity of ordinary American life, the Indians' cultivation of honor, courage, and the virtues familiar from military aristocracies in Europe exemplified for Tocqueville everything that democracies are in danger of losing. Nonetheless, there was no way of preventing it; to live alongside Europeans has everywhere been disastrous for native peoples. Even if the Europeans were determined to prevent the disaster, they would not know how.[16]

As to the black inhabitants of the United States,

Tocqueville was equally bleak. The situation of Negro slaves was obviously intolerable. Tocqueville's concern, however, was with the damage that the institution of slavery did to the white inhabitants of America. His bleakness reflected his sense of the impossibility of achieving any happy outcome, with or without emancipation. His argument about the demoralizing effect of slavery on the slave-owning society was not novel; but his exposition of it was much enlivened by the fact that he had, at great peril, traveled down the Ohio and could see the achievements of slavery on one bank of the river and those of free labor on the other. It was clear to him that the states where slavery was dominant were doomed to backwardness; in absolute terms, they might be more prosperous than most European countries, but they would not feel so, because their northern neighbors would be so much more prosperous than they.[17]

Tocqueville has been rightly admired by sociologists for his insistence that it is not absolute but comparative levels of well-being that determine whether a population is happy or resentful. Just as American patriotism is enhanced by the fact that immigrants compare their American present with their European past, southerners will increasingly resent the superior standard of living of northerners. The danger was that the white population in the slave states would be concerned only to preserve its superiority to its Negro serfs and would acquire all the bad habits of a decadent aristocracy. Meanwhile, the states where free labor was the rule would thrive and prosper; manufacturing cities would spring up, and their banks and trading companies would profit not only from the efforts of the free states but from those of the slave states, too. Such a state of affairs could not continue indefinitely, and whether it would spell the end of the United States was anyone's guess. The misery for the black slaves was that emancipation would do them little good. Northerners were opposed to slavery but no more willing than their southern counterparts to live alongside and intermarry with freed Negro slaves. Second-class citizenship and social apartheid would be the lot of freed slaves.

Tocqueville did not foresee the Civil War, although his letters to American correspondents after 1840 become increasingly unhappy as tensions between the northern and the southern states increased.[18] Nor was slavery the only cause of potential disunion that he mentioned, either in *Democracy* or in his letters. It is often said that he paid too little attention to the impact of Andrew Jackson's presidency and the arrival in the United States of the ethos of *enrichissez-vous* that Louis-Philippe brought to France. This is not quite just. In the middle of the discussion of the impact of slavery on American political cohesion, Tocqueville breaks off to observe that the center of gravity of the United States is inexorably shifting to the Mississippi basin. What concerns him about that fact is the character of the men who are thrusting westward from the eastern states. They are brash, impatient, headstrong, uninterested in the politics of the states from which they have emerged or have been expelled; a few years earlier, they had inspired American commentators to wonder whether civilized Americans tended to degenerate in the wilderness. The frontier is a double-edged feature of American life; it aids cohesion because it offers a safety valve for restless spirits, and the possibility of redemption for individuals whose first gambles have failed; on the other hand, it removes the restless, the ill disciplined, the impatient, and the reckless from the disciplining effects of a settled environment. If such people form the majority of the American population in forty years' time, chaos may be the young democracy's lot. But those fears came to haunt Tocqueville in the 1850s, not in the 1830s.

DEMOCRACY TWO

After reading the first volume of *Democracy*, one might wonder what was left to say about America. Tocqueville was sure there was much. The division of intellectual labor between the two volumes is not obvious, but four topics have been salient in the minds of commentators for the past half century. The first is Tocqueville's ambivalence about individualism and individuality, a subject that reappeared in American sociology after World War II in David Riesman's *The Lonely Crowd* and two decades later in Richard Sennett's *The Fall of Public Man*. The second is Tocqueville's discussion of the American genius for association, the third his thoughts on the family, and the fourth his vision of "soft despotism."

Tocqueville did not mince his words about American cultural life. He thought democracies unsuited to the production of high culture, and regarded American life as both frenetic and monotonous, a view held by most European visitors. He did not think much of the rhetorical abilities of American statesmen, and although the Americans were practical Cartesians, he did not think they could produce great American philosophers—as, of course, they did, with Peirce, James, and Dewey at the end of the century. American readers do not flinch at this unkindness. What unnerves them is the discussion of individualism. Tocqueville believed that the effect of equality was to make Americans more enthusiastic for equality than for freedom. This is the underlying theme of the second volume of *Democracy*, and its implications are everywhere.

INDIVIDUALISM AND RETREAT

Tocqueville was one the first writers to use the word "individualism"; he gave it a very particular meaning. It is the polar opposite of "individuality," understood as a strong sense of our own identity and the confidence to make something of ourselves that Mill praises in *On Liberty*. Tocqueville is diagnosing the feeling that leads Americans to turn away from the public realm and inward on themselves. It "is a reflective and peaceable sentiment that disposes each citizen to isolate himself from the mass of those like him, and to withdraw to one side with his family and friends, so that after having thus created a little society for his own use, he willingly abandons society at large to itself."[19] By the end of the short chapter in which this account appears, the world that the citizen, a citizen only in name, has retreated to has shrunk yet further. The process of retreat threatens to "confine him wholly in the solitude of his own heart." This is the image of the lonely crowd, of which so much was later made. Tocqueville does not draw on elaborate psychological theories to explain this retreat from the outside world. It is a retreat from the public world into the domestic world; it is not a manifestation of selfishness but a retreat from engagement.

This incapacity to engage with public affairs and politics is what Tocqueville fears almost more than anything else. These anxieties are more directly political than they became when Mill took them up and made them the foundation of *On Liberty*. Mill wanted individuals to make of themselves everything they could: to think for themselves and each to live her or his life through and through as their own project. Tocqueville's concern was political; he wanted to see fully engaged citizens, not docile breadwinners, but he was more accepting than Mill of the ordinary disciplines of social life. Admirers of Tocqueville emphasize that he thought a considerable degree of social conservatism was required for political liberalism to be possible. Mill did not. So eloquent was Tocqueville in depicting what *might* be the fate of American democracy that readers often fail to notice that he did not suggest that America had already succumbed to individualism. He set out both the dangers if the pressure to retreat into our domestic surroundings was not resisted, and the forces that provided such resistance. The first of these was the American capacity for association; and its analysis rested on another of Tocqueville's legacies to the sociology of democratic societies, the concept of "self-interest rightly understood."[20]

ASSOCIATION AND "SELF-INTEREST RIGHTLY UNDERSTOOD"

Tocqueville was amazed by the way Americans set up societies and clubs and associations to accomplish almost anything one could think of; by the time he wrote volume 2 of *Democracy*, he had visited Britain, but although America drew its laws and traditions from Britain, there was nothing in British life to match the American enthusiasm for setting up associations. It was not associations with a directly political object such as political parties that impressed him, but those that existed for nonpolitical purposes. Indeed, one frequent complaint against *Democracy* is that it ignores political parties, as indeed it does apart from a brief history of the Federalist and Republican parties. Establishing a school or college, building churches, sending missionaries all over the globe, and creating hospitals and prisons were all the object of associations large and small. Their existence was vital to American democracy: in a society where there were no aristocrats and therefore no natural leaders, and individuals had to cooperate with one another to achieve almost anything, associations were the cradle of democratic self-reliance. Tocqueville's habit of arguing by antithesis is very much in evidence.

Following Montesquieu, he saw the natural political condition of a society of equals as a tyranny, where a single despot ruled a state that controlled individuals who lacked the power to resist and had no way of organizing themselves to do so. America was the reverse of such a society. Nonpolitical associations fostered the skills of government, so that America was a genuinely self-governing republic. But if the state were to intervene to take over what was done by voluntary association, the spark that kept freedom alive might be extinguished. Tocqueville's antipathy to measures of relief in 1848, such as the national workshops proposed by Louis Blanc, rested largely on bad economics, but it also rested on a better, if not wholly persuasive, sociology.

Much of the impetus behind the creation of associations to achieve the diverse ends they aimed at came from a form of self-interest that Tocqueville approved of. This was "self-interest rightly understood." Tocqueville thought of this as a force that counteracted individualism. It seems odd to suggest that self-interest counteracts individualism, but once we see what is involved in "rightly understood," it is not. Tocqueville thought that Americans understood that in the absence of an interfering and omnicompetent state, they must manage their own affairs. If they wished their children to have an education, for instance, they must get together with like-minded people and build a school. This is self-interest with an eye to long-run, shared interests. The danger was that individuals would eventually give in to the temptation to have the state do everything for them; it was the natural path of a democracy to look for uniform solutions and centralize power for the purpose, but thus far Americans had resisted. The implications for the French, who had no such tradition of self-help, needed no spelling out.

So we have what became the canonical view of the dangers confronting democracy, and the raw materials for the continuing American anxiety about preserving the delicate balance between the private and the public realms. That anxiety was not drawn from a reading of Tocqueville alone, but he articulated it as eloquently as anyone. It is a platitude that if everyone withdraws into the pursuit of a privatized well-being, there will be no energy to fuel voluntary associations or to inspire the active membership of political parties—which are voluntary associations even if their purpose is to lay hold of the coercive mechanisms of the state. The nonplatitudinous element is partly moral—a question of how hard we should press the citizenry to participate—and partly factual—whether we are threatened by a decline in association. It may be that we blame a lack of civic engagement for things that have no connection to it. Behind these questions lies a normative vision of the engaged citizen that is taken for granted by political theorists such as Tocqueville and modern commentators, but that other writers have disputed. Burke would have thought that ordinary people should get on with their lives untroubled by politics; Plato would have gone much further to make sure they remained unengaged. Tocqueville thought Plato and Burke had been worsted by history. The world had fallen into the hands of the ordinary man and woman; the question was whether they could meet its challenges.

THE FAMILY

He therefore turned to the way in which the American family socialized the next generation of citizens. Tocqueville was tougher and bleaker than his modern admirers. With the French Revolution a near memory rather than old history, he emphasized the need for social discipline. He thought the modern world was gentler and more humane than the society of the ancien régime, where arbitrary and disgusting brutalities were perpetrated on political and religious dissenters, let alone on thieves and forgers.[21] The gentleness of the legal regime meant that self-discipline was all the more important, and it could be inculcated only in the family. Tocqueville's concern with the way the next generation was socialized into membership of a democratic society and polity led him to focus intensely on the role of women in American life: "There have never been free societies without *moeurs* . . . and it is woman who makes *moeurs*."[22] But women were located within the family, so Tocqueville's first move was to sketch the democratic family, and then the place of women in the family and the wider society.

The democratic family is contrasted with the aristocratic family. The latter is extended, the former nuclear; the idea of a lineage is un-American. Beyond a child's earliest years, relations within the family are based on friendship rather than authority. This is most vividly true of relationships between fathers and sons, but also of relations between siblings. In an aristocratic family, every person has a rank in the family hierarchy, which is perhaps a youngest son's observation. In a democratic family, children are friendly equals. But it is on American women that the preservation of good morals depends. This thought echoes Pericles and Polybius almost as loudly as Montesquieu. The remarkable feature of the upbringing of American girls was that they had absolute liberty until marriage, but liberty within a strict moral framework. One might glimpse between the lines Tocqueville's liking for young women who knew how to flirt without luring him into dangerous entanglements. Their political role stems from the most

remarkable feature of American marriage: absolute freedom before marriage was succeeded within marriage by
a strict, self-imposed subordination to its duties and the
welfare of the family. The hectic quality of American
life demanded a stabilizing force, and it was provided
by American women. They held families together in
misfortune, and kept their husbands on the path of
steady self-reliance. One healthy result was that Americans rated women at their true value as rational creatures and cooperative helpmates, while Europeans
exaggerated the seductive power of women, but treated
them as incapable of rational reflection.

SOFT DESPOTISM

America's success at balancing liberty and equality raised
the question whether the mores of the Americans could
protect them forever from the dangers of democratic tyranny. This is the topic about which Tocqueville wrote
most anxiously in both parts of *Democracy*. In the second
volume he spelled out an idea that became part of a permanent legacy of deep philosophical anxieties about the
fate of liberal democracies in the twentieth century. He
feared, he said, a form of despotism unlike anything
that had preceded it. Democracies were capable of cruelty and brutality for short periods; violence was not

foreign to them; but brutality and violence were not part of their nature. Their morality was mild, and their *moeurs* softer than those of an aristocratic or monarchical society. They were not likely to fall into the hands of tyrants in the traditional sense. What they had to fear was that their leaders would be schoolmasters, not despots, and this thought took Tocqueville back to his fears about "individualism" in the sense in which he had earlier defined it. Each individual would shrink, his boundaries confined to his family and a few friends. Above this mass of tiny individuals "an immense tutelary power is elevated."[23]

Paradoxically, this tutelary power is the collective power of all the tiny individuals in the aggregate; for this is majority tyranny in a social rather than a narrowly political context. Tocqueville relies on the contrast with what one might call standard tyranny. Here a sole ruler, violent, brutal, selfish, and careless of legality, exercises power by the application of brute force and physical terror. Before the rise of the modern totalitarian state, such rulers were terrifying if one was within range, ineffective if one was not. Traditional tyrants were like cannon firing high explosive into the countryside; if the shell landed where you were standing, you were dead, if not, life went on undisturbed. Democratic despotism is "soft" or "mild," but it is uniform, omnipresent, and inescapable. In a memorable and much

quoted phrase, Tocqueville says of it, "It does not tyrannize, it hinders, compromises, enervates, dazes, and
finally reduces each nation to being nothing more than
a herd of timid and industrious animals of which the
government is the shepherd."[24] This is the fear that
Mill expressed in *On Liberty*, and to which Aldous Hux-
ley gave a dramatic twist in *Brave New World*. In contemporary American politics, it looms large in the
imagination of the enemies of "big government," and
strikes others as absurdly exaggerated.

Whether there is any long-term remedy is a large
question. Tocqueville tells us what can certainly delay the
process, perhaps forever; it is the pluralism that represents the mirror image of the French centralization that
plays a prominent role in *L'ancien régime*. Tocqueville
believed that democracy had an inbuilt tendency toward
centralization. Aristocracies in contrast were innately
and multiply pluralistic: along intellectual, geographical,
social, economic dimensions. Critics might think the
diversity of status and function in aristocratic societies
came at too high a price; the difference of lifestyle between
starving peasant and overfed bishop was genuine but not
worth preserving. Tocqueville does not demur; but he
insists that aristocratic societies can preserve kinds of
freedom that more egalitarian societies would struggle to
protect. This tenderness toward the old aristocratic order

led Mill to remark, "You are much more drawn to the past than I am."[25] How far Tocqueville's anxieties were justified is contentious. In many respects, American society became more pluralistic as the nineteenth century wore on. White America was no longer Anglo-American, but embraced innumerable other European immigrants, including Catholics from Ireland, Italy, and southern and eastern Europe, followed by Jews fleeing Russian pogroms and oppression elsewhere; the opening of the Far West brought in Asian laborers, and the country picked up a substantial Mexican population by conquest, and drew in more by migration. The United States continued, as it still continues, to strike some Europeans as conformist and inhospitable to intellectual independence. Other observers are as impressed as ever by the country's astonishing inventiveness, scientific, technical, and cultural. What the aristocratic Tocqueville would have made of it is another matter, but he ought to have been reassured that democracies can generate a plurality of tastes, ambitions, and allegiances as diverse as anything visible under the ancien régime. In any case, Tocqueville's fears were for France rather than America; the tutelary state was a not implausible extrapolation from an ancien régime state in nineteenth-century conditions. It was a very unlikely extrapolation from the American state of the 1830s.

FRANCE AND EMPIRE

Tocqueville never wrote anything on French imperialism to match his investigation of what British imperialism had achieved in North America, but throughout *Democracy* he raises the question of why the French failed to match the British in establishing themselves overseas. The interest of his ideas, which are scattered in articles he wrote during his time in the National Assembly and two reports on a visit to Algeria in the early 1840s, is how different a liberal he was from most English liberals, Mill among them. Mill worked for the East India Company, which then ruled British India. He thought the British presence was justified by the good it could do to India; a progressive colonial power could accelerate economic, cultural, and political development as the native inhabitants could not. The question on which Mill was mostly silent was what the benefit to the imperial power was. Colonization, in the sense of settling Britons in Australia, New Zealand, and British North America, had an obvious purpose; Mill's economics depicted overpopulation as a constant danger for developed countries, and emigration was the safety valve. Imperialism as such did not stir his blood. Glory was not something he cared for; he admitted that a colonial empire conferred prestige on Britain, but in a less than enthusiastic tone.[26]

Tocqueville held very different views. He thought the French needed a grand national project to bring the country together, and the conquest and settlement of Algeria could be it. No more than Machiavelli did he think it was worth debating the morality of the matter. Tocqueville's brutal approach to the destruction of Kabyle and Arab villages, which amounted to the deliberate massacre of women and children in order to terrorize their menfolk into abandoning guerrilla war against the French, has shocked later readers. Shock is not the right reaction. Tocqueville was an educated man. He knew how harsh the establishment of imperial rule by Greeks, Romans, Ottomans, and the Spanish had been, and he did not flinch. Politics could not be constrained by squeamishness. Unlike Mill (and Marx), Tocqueville did not invoke a vision of the benefits of progress to justify the methods used to bring it about. Indeed, just as in the case of the American Indians, he was much more sensitive to what was lost than either Mill or Marx. What France would get from success in Algeria was national glory, an increase in self-confidence, and solidarity. This outlook underlay some incidental remarks in *Democracy*, where Tocqueville hopes that a growing American navy will ally itself with the French to check British supremacy. Tocqueville did not imagine that Britain and France would or should go to war again, but it was not good for French self-confidence to lag so spectacularly behind that neighbor.

THE ANCIEN RÉGIME

This discussion has focused on Tocqueville's anxieties about the future of liberal democracy, and what democracy in America suggested about its prospects in France. Like all commentators, Tocqueville emphasized that the Americans had not had to contend with the class hatreds left over from the ancien régime or with the unfinished business of the French Revolution, or even with the less obtrusive social hierarchies of Britain. The French Revolution had not only made it hard to establish a constitution—whether republican or monarchical—that would be widely accepted as legitimate but had made it almost impossible to reach a consensus on what a legitimate regime might look like. Between the undesired extremes of anarchy and a theocratic monarchy, there was much room for dissension and little hope of agreement. Like every reflective Frenchman, Tocqueville was fascinated by the revolution and its descent from a cautious movement for constitutional change into the madness of the Terror. For many years he thought of writing a history of the revolution itself; then he decided that to make sense of the events of the revolution, it was necessary to go back to the regime that the revolution had destroyed, and wrote his "third masterpiece," *L'ancien régime*. It is, like *Democracy*, a work of great richness, in which it is easy to lose oneself. Here I touch only on the aspects of the book that are directly reflected from *Democracy*.

Tocqueville's account of the French Revolution is justly famous for its refutation of the claim that it broke out because of the intolerable misery of the French people. Tocqueville employed what social scientists later called "reference group theory," the simple idea that whether we are content or unhappy depends on whom we compare ourselves with. The real work of the theory is done by answering the question of whom we take as the appropriate people with whom to compare ourselves. When this thought was applied to the United States, it suggested that immigrants who compared themselves with their poorer and more confined European selves felt happier than their objective conditions warranted, because they took their standards from their old lives and felt better-off as a result. It is frequently said today that many American who are objectively hard-up continue to think of themselves as "middle-class" because they compare themselves with their near neighbors rather than with Wall Street bankers. The theory suggests two things: first, that synchronically we compare ourselves with those with whom we come into contact, and accept or resent differences between them and us to the extent that we think there is some justice to those differences, or at least, no injustice; second, that diachronically we become very unhappy if we first begin to become prosperous and then find our path blocked, unhappier than if we had never started on the upward path.

In Tocqueville's view this second factor was the crucial one. The theory is summarized in a chapter heading: "How Efforts to Help the Masses Radicalized Them."[27] The situation an old-fashioned absolute monarchy had to avoid was provoking the bourgeoisie to side with the laboring classes; to do so when the aristocracy had too little loyalty to the regime to defend it with real vigor would be disastrous. The French monarchy had done it. It did it slowly and over a long period, and many other things had made the regime vulnerable, too. In the short term, the revolution spread rapidly because there had been successive failed harvests; but it was not the rural peasantry that stormed the Bastille. It was the Paris mob. It was led by artisans, but behind them lay the political interests of their social superiors. The leaders who emerged during the revolution were mostly members of the professional middle classes. It was not absurd for Marxists to claim that the French Revolution was a bourgeois revolution.

Looking for antithetical examples as always, Tocqueville pointed to Britain. Political power was in the hands of an elite, composed of the gentry, and frequently the sons of the nobility; but nobody expected revolution in Britain. Perhaps the English got the revolutionary virus out of their system by killing one king and driving another into exile, but that was hardly the explanation. Many English writers and political leaders were initially committed to the principles of the French Revolution, which was scarcely surprising when they were to all appearances the principles of 1688. Among them were republicans, rationalists, and democrats, as well as many Dissenters shut out of regular political life by the Test and Corporation Acts. They had no chance of creating in England anything resembling the upheavals in Paris; when the British government took repressive measures against domestic radicalism in the early 1790s, the public was firmly on the government's side. The government did not fear that the army might not obey orders, and had no doubt the courts would find its critics guilty of sedition when they were prosecuted. The French came within a whisper of executing Thomas Paine, but he would probably have been sentenced to death for sedition by a British court, if ministers had been able to prosecute him.

Tocqueville asked two large questions. Why was the French state so vulnerable, and why did the revolution simultaneously change everything and nothing? The vulnerabilities of the French state were innumerable, and by the time Tocqueville has finished explaining the ways in which it was a glittering sham, it is less of a surprise that it fell than that it survived so long. The central theme can be inferred from the reflections on democracy and despotism in the second volume of *Democracy*. In France the aristocracy had become useless; for the sake of increasing royal authority, the monarchy had over centuries reduced the aristocracy to political impotence. In compensation it had allowed it to retain and increase its financial privileges and to exercise an increasingly oppressive power over the peasantry. There were areas of France in which the peasantry was no better off in 1789 than in 1289. The political consequence was that the aristocracy was hated worse in France than elsewhere; feudal institutions not only seemed to have, but actually had, no function but to extract resources from the poor and transfer them to the rich. Since the aristocracy was functionless, its privileges were not a legitimate reward for the social tasks it performed. They were merely privileges. The common people were therefore ready whenever the chance might occur to overthrow the aristocratic regime.

One might think that in any society the worse-off would always be ready to help themselves to the possessions of the better-off; in urban riots there is always a lot of opportunistic looting, as there is in the country-side when villagers have the opportunity to loot a great house. Nonetheless, order only rarely breaks down, and in some societies, of which Tocqueville thought Britain was one, it is never in danger of wholly doing so. The defense against disorder and pillage is not armed force but giving enough people a stake in law and order and the protection of property. In a stable society where the hollowing out that the French state had suffered has not taken place, there is a steady gradation of prosperity from the better-off to the worse-off. The alluring prospect for the middle classes is that they or their children can make their way into the gentry and higher. This was not true in France. Tocqueville provided an interesting variation on the old theme that the aristocracy of Britain was ready to accept into its ranks those who made money from trade. It was not that one could not buy nobility in France; the purchase of an office achieved it. It was rather than the social boundaries of the English nobility were indistinct, which made "In or out?" a less painful question. In contrast, the aristocracy of France was a caste. The whole point of membership was social exclusiveness. The natural allies of an aristocratic regime became its bitterest enemies.[28]

Nonetheless, it astonished observers that an urban riot—the storming of the Bastille—could bring down the most powerful state in Europe. Tocqueville thought it not astonishing at all. The aristocracy had become parasitic, attached to its privileges and serving no social or political function. Unlike the English aristocracy, which lived on its estates and ran the legal and political machinery of the countryside, the French aristocracy was called to court to serve a decorative function. France became a centralized administrative despotism. If anyone wanted redress for a problem, no matter where he might live, it was to the agents of the royal administration that he had to address himself. Although London was disproportionately the largest and most vital city in England, it did not monopolize political authority, energy, and administrative capacity as Paris did. Much as the American colonies practiced their own familiar forms of self-government during the American Revolution, the British could have governed themselves, if London had been overwhelmed by some disaster. Not so the French. This explained the ease with which the revolution overthrew the ancien régime as well as the ease with which the revolutionaries maintained their power and the ease with which they lost it. Tocqueville quoted Burke's astonishment that during the revolution people were arrested for the most contradictory reasons and their neighbors never lifted a finger to help. Tocqueville thought this demonstrated Burke's failure to understand how completely the monarchy had dissolved the ties of affection, self-help, and initiative that Burke took for granted. The Americans had their habits of association and the principle of self-interest rightly understood to protect themselves against the atomization of an egalitarian society; the French did not.

Tocqueville and Burke are at one in their view of the disastrous consequence of French irreligion and the catastrophic rise of the deracinated intellectual that was the other face of increasing skepticism. Tocqueville thought it was a self-inflicted disaster on the part of the aristocracy. If aristocrats had understood the extent to which their position depended on the religious convictions of the rest of society, they would have refrained from sponsoring the intellectuals who mocked religion. The institutional church was no help; indeed, it was its own worst enemy. The senior clergy were aristocrats and attracted the same opprobrium as the rest of the aristocracy; the humble curé had no affection for the church hierarchy, and when the revolution came, the lowest ranks in the church were not sorry to see the hierarchy overthrown.

In Tocqueville's view, the weaknesses of the old regime also explain why everything and nothing was changed by the revolution. Before the revolution, administrative centralization had taken hold; the French had become uniform in their tastes, habits, and allegiances; they had come to expect the state to provide for the whole of life. This did not mean that they had no energy; smallholding peasants worked desperately hard and had great powers of endurance. What they did not have were the habits of association, the capacity to generate "bottom-up" loyalties rather than loyalty to the state, "top-down" allegiance. Because a passion for equality had taken hold before the revolution, all hereditary privileges were destined to be swept away; for a brief period a passion for freedom, self-rule, nondomination by the powers that be was strong. The violence and fury of the revolution reflected the fact that once the common people were liberated, they had no reason to respect the boundaries their erstwhile rulers took for granted. The increasing mildness of manners in the eighteenth century was consistent with the utter savagery of the revolution as it moved toward its explosive climax. But as soon as desire for tranquility overtook the urge to liberate themselves, postrevolutionary France returned to the political passivity of the ancien régime. It became what America had to ensure it did not become, an easy prey to despotic rulers such as Napoleon III.

Hegel, Mill, and Tocqueville are not usually yoked together; Hegel's reputation is for metaphysical inscrutability, Mill's for a lucidity of expression that fails to hide some deep uncertainties, and Tocqueville is more admired for what he is thought to have written about America in the 1830s than read with care. It would strain the reader's credulity to deny their differences.

Nonetheless, they mark a turning point in political thinking and in what are thought to be the crucial questions. This is the moment where liberals begin to ask how a socially egalitarian society can avoid being dominated by public opinion and the dead weight of the "mass," whether middle-class or lower-class, whether resentful and sullen or comfortably oppressive. The age-old question arises in a new form: whether the members of modern society can be citizens as well as subjects, practicing genuine self-government as well as enjoying the benefits of rational administration and the securities for a reasonable level of welfare that an efficient bureaucracy can provide. We know that the modern world is decisively different from the world of the ancients; we do not know which of their ideals and ambitions we must renounce with regret, and which we can recapture in modern forms, not least because we do not know how much effort we would be prepared to devote to the task, let alone how hard it would be. The new sense of how different the modern world had become from what went before also induced a deep uncertainty about how different it might become. Hegel, Mill, and Tocqueville refused to prophesy the future; and as to the means of social change, all were close enough to the French Revolution to think that violent insurrection was the method of last resort in effecting social change. Marx was another matter.

NOTES

1 Jennifer Pitts, *A Turn to Empire: The Rise of Imperial Liberalism in Britain and France* (Princeton: Princeton University Press, 2005), pp. 200ff.

2 André Jardin, *Tocqueville: A Biography*, trans. Lydia Davis, with Robert Hemenway (New York: Farrar Straus Giroux, 1988), pp. 88ff.

3 Ibid., pp. 52–53.

4 Translated as *Recollections*.

5 John Stuart Mill, *Letters*, in *The Collected Works of John Stuart Mill*, 32 vols. (Toronto: University of Toronto Press, 1963–96), 15:517–18.

6 Hugh Brogan, *Alexis de Tocqueville: A Life* (New Haven: Yale University Press, 2007), p. 501.

7 Alexis de Tocqueville, *Democracy in America*, ed. Isaac Kramnick, trans. Gerald Bevan (London: Penguin, 2003), vol. 1, p. 233.

8 Ibid., vol. 2, pp. 684–96.

9 Ibid., pp. 803ff.

10 John Stuart Mill, "The State of Society in America," in *Collected Works*, 18:98–100.

11 Tocqueville, *Democracy*, vol. 2, p. 494.

12 Ibid., vol. 1, pp. 14ff. ("Author's Introduction").

13 Ibid., p. 14–16.

14 Usefully collected in Aurelian Craiutu and Jeremy Jennings, eds., *Tocqueville on America after 1840: Letters*

and Other Writings (New York: Cambridge University Press, 2009).

15 Tocqueville, Democracy, vol. I, pp. 201–2, 223–34.

16 Ibid., pp. 391–97.

17 Ibid., pp. 405–6.

18 Craiutu and Jennings, eds., Tocqueville on America, pp. 26–39.

19 Tocqueville, Democracy, vol. 2, p. 587.

20 Ibid., pp. 591–600.

21 Ibid., p. 684.

22 Ibid.

23 Ibid., p. 805.

24 Ibid., p. 806.

25 Mill, Letters, in Collected Works, 15:518.

26 John Stuart Mill, Representative Government, in Collected Works, 19:565.

27 Alexis de Tocqueville, The Old Regime and the Revolution, ed. François Furet and Françoise Mélonio, trans. Alan S. Kahan, 2 vols. (Chicago: University of Chicago Press, 2001), pp. 225–30.

28 Ibid., pp. 156–60.

Selections

❦

DEMOCRACY IN AMERICA

Volume One

INTRODUCTORY CHAPTER

Amongst the novel objects that attracted my attention during my stay in the United States, nothing struck me more forcibly than the general equality of conditions. I readily discovered the prodigious influence which this primary fact exercises on the whole course of society, by giving a certain direction to public opinion, and a certain tenor to the laws; by imparting new maxims to the governing powers, and peculiar habits to the governed. I speedily perceived that the influence of this fact extends far beyond the political character and the laws of the country, and that it has no less empire over civil society than over the Government;

it creates opinions, engenders sentiments, suggests the ordinary practices of life, and modifies whatever it does not produce. The more I advanced in the study of American society, the more I perceived that the equality of conditions is the fundamental fact from which all others seem to be derived, and the central point at which all my observations constantly terminated.

I then turned my thoughts to our own hemisphere, where I imagined that I discerned something analogous to the spectacle which the New World presented to me. I observed that the equality of conditions is daily progressing towards those extreme limits which it seems to have reached in the United States, and that the democracy which governs the American communities appears to be rapidly rising into power in Europe. I hence conceived the idea of the book which is now before the reader.

It is evident to all alike that a great democratic revolution is going on amongst us; but there are two opinions as to its nature and consequences. To some it appears to be a novel accident, which as such may still be checked; to others it seems irresistible, because it is the most uniform, the most ancient, and the most permanent tendency which is to be found in history. . . .

. . . The various occurrences of national existence have everywhere turned to the advantage of democracy; all men have aided it by their exertions: those who have intentionally labored in its cause, and those who have served it unwittingly; those who have fought for it and those who have declared themselves its opponents, have all been driven along in the same track, have all labored to one end, some ignorantly and some unwillingly; all have been blind instruments in the hands of God.

The gradual development of the equality of conditions is a providential fact, and it possesses all the characteristics of a divine decree: it is universal, it is durable, it constantly eludes all human interference, and all events as well as all men contribute to its progress. Would it, then, be wise to imagine that a social impulse which dates from so far back can be checked by the efforts of a generation? Is it credible that the democracy which has annihilated the feudal system and vanquished kings will respect the citizen and the capitalist? Will it stop now that it has grown so strong and its adversaries so weak? None can say which way we are going, for all terms of comparison are wanting: the equality of conditions is more complete in the Christian countries of the present day than it has been at any time or in any part of the world; so that the extent of what already exists prevents us from foreseeing what may be yet to come.

The whole book which is here offered to the public has been written under the impression of a kind of religious dread produced in the author's mind by the contemplation of so irresistible a revolution, which has

advanced for centuries in spite of such amazing obstacles, and which is still proceeding in the midst of the
ruins it has made. It is not necessary that God himself
should speak in order to disclose to us the unquestion-
able signs of His will; we can discern them in the habitual course of nature, and in the invariable tendency of
events: I know, without a special revelation, that the
planets move in the orbits traced by the Creator's finger.
If the men of our time were led by attentive observation
and by sincere reflection to acknowledge that the gradual and progressive development of social equality is at
once the past and future of their history, this solitary
truth would confer the sacred character of a Divine
decree upon the change. To attempt to check democracy would be in that case to resist the will of God; and
the nations would then be constrained to make the best
of the social lot awarded to them by Providence.

The Christian nations of our age seem to me to present a most alarming spectacle; the impulse which is
bearing them along is so strong that it cannot be stopped,
but it is not yet so rapid that it cannot be guided: their
fate is in their hands; yet a little while and it may be so
no longer. The first duty which is at this time imposed
upon those who direct our affairs is to educate the
democracy; to warm its faith, if that be possible; to
purify its morals; to direct its energies; to substitute a
knowledge of business for its inexperience, and an

acquaintance with its true interests for its blind propensities; to adapt its government to time and place, and to modify it in compliance with the occurrences and the actors of the age. A new science of politics is indispensable to a new world. This, however, is what we think of least; launched in the middle of a rapid stream, we obstinately fix our eyes on the ruins which may still be descried upon the shore we have left, whilst the current sweeps us along, and drives us backwards towards the gulf. . . .

There is a country in the world where the great revolution which I am speaking of seems nearly to have reached its natural limits; it has been effected with ease and simplicity, say rather that this country has attained the consequences of the democratic revolution which we are undergoing without having experienced the revolution itself. The emigrants who fixed themselves on the shores of America in the beginning of the seventeenth century severed the democratic principle from all the principles which repressed it in the old communities of Europe, and transplanted it unalloyed to the New World. It has there been allowed to spread in perfect freedom, and to put forth its consequences in the laws by influencing the manners of the country.

It appears to me beyond a doubt that sooner or later we shall arrive, like the Americans, at an almost complete equality of conditions. But I do not conclude from this that we shall ever be necessarily led to draw the same political consequences which the Americans have derived from a similar social organization. I am far from supposing that they have chosen the only form of government which a democracy may adopt; but the identity of the efficient cause of laws and manners in the two countries is sufficient to account for the immense interest we have in becoming acquainted with its effects in each of them.

It is not, then, merely to satisfy a legitimate curiosity that I have examined America; my wish has been to find instruction by which we may ourselves profit. Whoever should imagine that I have intended to write a panegyric will perceive that such was not my design; nor has it been my object to advocate any form of government in particular, for I am of opinion that absolute excellence is rarely to be found in any legislation; I have not even affected to discuss whether the social revolution, which I believe to be irresistible, is advantageous or prejudicial to mankind; I have acknowledged this revolution as a fact already accomplished or on the eve of its accomplishment; and I have selected the nation, from amongst those which have undergone it, in which its development has been the most peaceful and the most complete, in order to discern its natural consequences, and, if it be possible, to distinguish the means by which it may be rendered profitable. I confess that in America I saw more than America; I sought the image of democracy itself, with its inclinations, its character, its prejudices, and its passions, in order to learn what we have to fear or to hope from its progress. . . .

Part One

Chapter III

SOCIAL CONDITIONS OF THE ANGLO-AMERICANS

. . . Many important observations suggest themselves upon the social condition of the Anglo-Americans, but there is one which takes precedence of all the rest. The social condition of the Americans is eminently democratic; this was its character at the foundation of the Colonies, and is still more strongly marked at the present day. I have stated in the preceding chapter that great equality existed among the emigrants who settled on the shores of New England. The germ of aristocracy was never planted in that part of the union. The only influence which obtained there was that of intellect; the people were used to reverence certain names as the emblems of knowledge and virtue. Some of their fellow-citizens acquired a power over the rest which might truly have been called aristocratic, if it had been capable of transmission from father to son.

This was the state of things to the east of the Hudson: to the south-west of that river, and in the direction of the Floridas, the case was different. In most of the states situated to the south-west of the Hudson some great English proprietors had settled, who had imported with them aristocratic principles and the English law of descent. I have explained the reasons why it was impossible ever to establish a powerful aristocracy in America; these reasons existed with less force to the south-west of the Hudson. In the south, one man, aided by slaves, could cultivate a great extent of country: it was therefore common to see rich landed proprietors. But their influence was not altogether aristocratic as that term is understood in Europe, since they possessed no privileges; and the cultivation of their estates being carried on by slaves, they had no tenants depending on them, and consequently no patronage. Still, the great proprietors south of the Hudson constituted a superior class, having ideas and tastes of its own, and forming the centre of political action. This kind of aristocracy sympathized with the body of the people, whose passions and interests it easily embraced; but it was too weak and too short-lived to excite either love or hatred for itself. This was the class which headed the insurrection in the south, and furnished the best leaders of the American revolution. . . .

I do not mean that there is any deficiency of wealthy individuals in the United States; I know of no country, indeed, where the love of money has taken stronger hold on the affections of men, and where the profounder contempt is expressed for the theory of the permanent equality of property. But wealth circulates with inconceivable rapidity, and experience shows that it is rare to find two succeeding generations in the full enjoyment of it.

This picture, which may perhaps be thought to be overcharged, still gives a very imperfect idea of what is taking place in the new states of the west and southwest. At the end of the last century a few bold adventurers began to penetrate into the valleys of the Mississippi, and the mass of the population very soon began to move in that direction: communities unheard of till then were seen to emerge from the wilds: states whose names were not in existence a few years before claimed their place in the American union; and in the western settlements we may behold democracy arrived at its utmost extreme. In these states, founded off-hand, and, as it were, by chance, the inhabitants are but of yesterday. Scarcely known to one another, the nearest neighbors are ignorant of each other's history. In this part of the American continent, therefore, the population has not experienced the influence of great names and great wealth, nor even that of the natural aristocracy of knowledge and virtue. None are there to wield that respectable power which men willingly grant to the remembrance of a life spent in doing good before their eyes. The new states of the west are already inhabited, but society has no existence among them.

It is not only the fortunes of men which are equal in America; even their requirements partake in some degree of the same uniformity. I do not believe that there is a country in the world where, in proportion to the population, there are so few uninstructed and at the same time so few learned individuals. Primary instruction is within the reach of everybody; superior instruction is scarcely to be obtained by any. This is not surprising; it is in fact the necessary consequence of what we have advanced above. Almost all the Americans are in easy circumstances, and can therefore obtain the first elements of human knowledge.

There is no class, then, in America, in which the taste for intellectual pleasures is transmitted with hereditary fortune and leisure, and by which the labors of the intellect are held in honor. Accordingly there is an equal want of the desire and the power of application to these objects.

A middle standard is fixed in America for human knowledge. All approach as near to it as they can; some as they rise, others as they descend. Of course, an immense multitude of persons are to be found who entertain the same number of ideas on religion, history, science, political economy, legislation, and government. The gifts of intellect proceed directly from God, and man cannot prevent their unequal distribution. But in consequence of the state of things which we have here represented it happens that, although the capacities of men are widely different, as the Creator has doubtless intended they should be, they are submitted to the same method of treatment.

In America the aristocratic element has always been feeble from its birth; and if at the present day it is not actually destroyed, it is at any rate so completely disabled that we can scarcely assign to it any degree of influence in the course of affairs. The democratic principle, on the contrary, has gained so much strength by time, by events, and by legislation, as to have become not only predominant but all-powerful. There is no family or corporate authority, and it is rare to find even the influence of individual character enjoy any durability.

America, then, exhibits in her social state a most extraordinary phenomenon. Men are there seen on a greater equality in point of fortune and intellect, or, in other words, more equal in their strength, than in any other country of the world, or in any age of which history has preserved the remembrance.

The political consequences of such a social condition as this are easily deducible. It is impossible to believe that equality will not eventually find its way into the political world as it does everywhere else. To conceive of men remaining forever unequal upon one single point, yet equal on all others, is impossible; they must come in the end to be equal upon all. Now I know of only two methods of establishing equality in the political world; every citizen must be put in possession of his rights, or rights must be granted to no one. For nations which are arrived at the same stage of social existence as the Anglo-Americans, it is therefore very difficult to discover a medium between the sovereignty of all and the absolute power of one man: and it would be vain to deny that the social condition which I have been describing is equally liable to each of these consequences.

There is, in fact, a manly and lawful passion for equality which excites men to wish all to be powerful and honored. This passion tends to elevate the humble to the rank of the great; but there exists also in the human heart a depraved taste for equality, which impels the weak to attempt to lower the powerful to their own level, and reduces men to prefer equality in slavery to inequality with freedom. Not that those nations whose social condition is democratic naturally despise liberty; on the contrary, they have an instinctive love of it. But liberty is not the chief and constant object of their desires; equality is their idol: they make rapid and sudden efforts to obtain liberty, and if they miss their aim resign themselves to their disappointment; but nothing can satisfy them except equality, and rather than lose it they resolve to perish.

On the other hand, in a state where the citizens are

nearly on an equality, it becomes difficult for them to preserve their independence against the aggressions of power. No one among them being strong enough to engage in the struggle with advantage, nothing but a general combination can protect their liberty. And such a union is not always to be found.

From the same social position, then, nations may derive one or the other of two great political results; these results are extremely different from each other, but they may both proceed from the same cause.

The Anglo-Americans are the first nations who, having been exposed to this formidable alternative, have been happy enough to escape the dominion of absolute power. They have been allowed by their circumstances, their origin, their intelligence, and especially by their moral feeling, to establish and maintain the sovereignty of the people.

Chapter IV

THE PRINCIPLE OF THE SOVEREIGNTY OF THE PEOPLE IN AMERICA

Whenever the political laws of the United States are to be discussed, it is with the doctrine of the sovereignty of the people that we must begin. The principle of the sovereignty of the people, which is to be found, more or less, at the bottom of almost all human institutions, generally remains concealed from view. It is obeyed without being recognized, or if for a moment it be brought to light, it is hastily cast back into the gloom of the sanctuary. "The will of the nation" is one of those expressions which have been most profusely abused by the wily and the despotic of every age. To the eyes of some it has been represented by the venal suffrages of a few of the satellites of power; to others by the votes of a timid or an interested minority; and some have even discovered it in the silence of a people, on the supposition that the fact of submission established the right of command.

In America the principle of the sovereignty of the people is not either barren or concealed, as it is with some other nations; it is recognized by the customs and proclaimed by the laws; it spreads freely, and arrives without impediment at its most remote consequences. If there be a country in the world where the doctrine of the sovereignty of the people can be fairly appreciated, where it can be studied in its application to the affairs of society, and where its dangers and its advantages may be foreseen, that country is assuredly America.

I have already observed that, from their origin, the sovereignty of the people was the fundamental principle of the greater number of British colonies in America. It was far, however, from then exercising as much influence on the government of society as it now does. Two obstacles, the one external, the other internal, checked its invasive progress. It could not ostensibly disclose itself in the laws of colonies which were still constrained to obey the mother-country: it was therefore obliged to spread secretly, and to gain ground in the provincial assemblies, and especially in the townships.

The American revolution broke out, and the doctrine of the sovereignty of the people, which had been nurtured in the townships and municipalities, took possession of the state: every class was enlisted in its cause; battles were fought, and victories obtained for it, until it became the law of laws. . . .

At the present day the principle of the sovereignty of the people has acquired, in the United States, all the practical development which the imagination can conceive. It is unencumbered by those fictions which have been thrown over it in other countries, and it appears in every possible form according to the exigency of the occasion. Sometimes the laws are made by the people in a body, as at Athens; and sometimes its representatives, chosen by universal suffrage, transact business in its name, and almost under its immediate control.

In some countries a power exists which, though it is in a degree foreign to the social body, directs it, and forces it to pursue a certain track. In others the ruling force is divided, being partly within and partly without the ranks of the people. But nothing of the kind is to be seen in the United States; there society governs itself for itself. All power centres in its bosom; and scarcely an individual is to be meet with who would venture to conceive, or, still less, to express, the idea of seeking it elsewhere. The nation participates in the making of its laws by the choice of its legislators, and in the execution of them by the choice of the agents of the executive government; it may almost be said to govern itself, so feeble and so restricted is the share left to the administration, so little do the authorities forget their popular origin and the power from which they emanate.

Chapter IX

WHY THE PEOPLE MAY STRICTLY BE SAID
TO GOVERN IN THE UNITED STATES

. . . In America the people appoints the legislative and the executive power, and furnishes the jurors who punish all offences against the laws. The American institutions are democratic, not only in their principle but in all their consequences; and the people elects its representatives directly, and for the most part annually, in order to ensure their dependence. The people is therefore the real directing power; and although the form of government is representative, it is evident that the opinions, the prejudices, the interests, and even the passions of the community are hindered by no durable obstacles from exercising a perpetual influence on society. In the United States the majority governs in the name of the people, as is the case in all the countries in which the people is supreme. The majority is principally composed of peaceful citizens who, either by inclination or by interest, are sincerely desirous of the welfare of their country. But they are surrounded by the incessant agitation of parties, which attempt to gain their co-operation and to avail themselves of their support.

Part Two

Chapter VI

ADVANTAGES AMERICAN SOCIETY

DERIVES FROM DEMOCRACY

. . . The defects and the weaknesses of a democratic government may very readily be discovered; they are demonstrated by the most flagrant instances, whilst its beneficial influence is less perceptibly exercised. A single glance suffices to detect its evil consequences, but its good qualities can only be discerned by long observation. The laws of the American democracy are frequently defective or incomplete; they sometimes attack vested rights, or give a sanction to others which are dangerous to the community; but even if they were good, the frequent changes which they undergo would be an evil. How comes it, then, that the American republics prosper and maintain their position?

In the consideration of laws a distinction must be carefully observed between the end at which they aim and the means by which they are directed to that end, between their absolute and their relative excellence. If it be the intention of the legislator to favor the interests of the minority at the expense of the majority, and if the measures he takes are so combined as to accomplish the object he has in view with the least possible expense of time and exertion, the law may be well drawn up, although its purpose be bad; and the more efficacious it is, the greater is the mischief which it causes.

Democratic laws generally tend to promote the welfare of the greatest possible number; for they emanate from the majority of the citizens, who are subject to error, but who cannot have an interest opposed to their own advantage. The laws of an aristocracy tend, on the contrary, to concentrate wealth and power in the hands of the minority, because an aristocracy, by its very nature, constitutes a minority. It may therefore be asserted, as a general proposition, that the purpose of a democracy in the conduct of its legislation is useful to a greater number of citizens than that of an aristocracy. This is, however, the sum total of its advantages.

Aristocracies are infinitely more expert in the science of legislation than democracies ever can be. They are possessed of a self-control which protects them from the errors of temporary excitement, and they form lasting designs which they mature with the assistance of favorable opportunities. Aristocratic government proceeds with the dexterity of art; it understands how to make the collective force of all its laws converge at the same time to a given point. Such is not the case with democracies, whose laws are almost always ineffective or inopportune. The means of democracy are therefore more imperfect than those of aristocracy, and the measures which it unwittingly adopts are frequently opposed to its own cause; but the object it has in view is more useful.

Let us now imagine a community so organized by nature, or by its constitution, that it can support the transitory action of bad laws, and that it can await, without destruction, the general tendency of the legislation: we shall then be able to conceive that a democratic government, notwithstanding its defects, will be most fitted to conduce to the prosperity of this community. This is precisely what has occurred in the United States; and I repeat, what I have before remarked, that the great advantage of the Americans consists in their being able to commit faults which they may afterward repair.

An analogous observation may be made respecting public officers. It is easy to perceive that the American democracy frequently errs in the choice of the individuals to whom it entrusts the power of the administration; but it is more difficult to say why the state prospers under their rule. In the first place it is to be remarked, that if in a democratic state the governors have less honesty and less capacity than elsewhere, the governed, on the other hand, are more enlightened and more attentive to their interests. As the people in democracies is more incessantly vigilant in its affairs and more jealous of its rights, it prevents its representatives from abandoning that general line of conduct which its own interest prescribes. In the second place, it must be remembered that if the democratic magistrate is more apt to misuse his power, he possesses it for a shorter period of time. But there is yet another reason which is still more general and conclusive. It is no doubt of importance to the welfare of nations that they should be governed by men of talents and virtue; but it is perhaps still more important that the interests of those men should not differ from the interests of the community at large; for, if such were the case, virtues of a high order might become useless, and talents might be turned to a bad account. I say that it is important that the interests of the persons in authority should not conflict with or oppose the interests of the community at large; but I do not insist upon their having the same interests as the whole population, because I am not aware that such a state of things ever existed in any country. . . .

The men who are entrusted with the direction of public affairs in the United States are frequently inferior, both in point of capacity and of morality, to those whom aristocratic institutions would raise to power. But their interest is identified and confounded with that of the majority of their fellow-citizens. They may frequently be faithless and frequently mistaken, but they will never systematically adopt a line of conduct opposed to the will of the majority; and it is impossible that they should give a dangerous or an exclusive tendency to the government.

The mal-administration of a democratic magistrate is a mere isolated fact, which only occurs during the short period for which he is elected. Corruption and incapacity do not act as common interests, which may connect men permanently with one another. A corrupt or an incapable magistrate will not concert his measures with another magistrate, simply because that individual is as corrupt and as incapable as himself; and these two men will never unite their endeavors to promote the corruption and inaptitude of their remote posterity. The ambition and the manoeuvres of the one will serve, on the contrary, to unmask the other. The vices of a magistrate, in democratic states, are usually peculiar to his own person.

But under aristocratic governments public men are swayed by the interest of their order, which, if it is sometimes confounded with the interests of the majority, is very frequently distinct from them. This interest is the common and lasting bond which unites them together; it induces them to coalesce, and to combine their efforts in order to attain an end which does not always ensure the greatest happiness of the greatest number; and it serves not only to connect the persons in authority, but to unite them to a considerable portion of the community, since a numerous body of citizens belongs to the aristocracy, without being invested with official functions. The aristocratic magistrate is therefore constantly supported by a portion of the community, as well as by the government of which he is a member.

The common purpose which connects the interest of the magistrates in aristocracies with that of a portion of their contemporaries identifies it with that of future generations; their influence belongs to the future as much as to the present. The aristocratic magistrate is urged at the same time toward the same point by the passions of the community, by his own, and I may almost add by those of his posterity. Is it, then, wonderful that he does not resist such repeated impulses? And indeed aristocracies are often carried away by the spirit of their order without being corrupted by it; and they unconsciously fashion society to their own ends, and prepare it for their own descendants. . . .

In the United States, where the public officers have no interests to promote connected with their caste, the general and constant influence of the government is beneficial, although the individuals who conduct it are frequently unskilful and sometimes contemptible. There is indeed a secret tendency in democratic institutions to render the exertions of the citizens subservient to the prosperity of the community, notwithstanding their private vices and mistakes; whilst in aristocratic institutions there is a secret propensity which, notwithstanding the talents and the virtues of those who conduct the government, leads them to contribute to the evils which oppress their fellow-creatures. In aristocratic governments public men may frequently do injuries which they do not intend, and in democratic states they produce advantages which they never thought of.

There is one sort of patriotic attachment which principally arises from that instinctive, disinterested, and undefinable feeling which connects the affections of man with his birthplace. This natural fondness is united to a taste for ancient customs, and to a reverence for ancestral traditions of the past; those who cherish it love their country as they love the mansions of their fathers. They enjoy the tranquillity which it affords them; they cling to the peaceful habits which they have contracted within its bosom; they are attached to the reminiscences which it awakens, and they are even pleased by the state of obedience in which they are placed. This patriotism is sometimes stimulated by religious enthusiasm, and then it is capable of making the most prodigious efforts. It is in itself a kind of religion; it does not reason, but it acts from the impulse of faith and of sentiment. By some nations the monarch has been regarded as a personification of the country; and the fervor of patriotism being converted into the fervor of loyalty, they took a sympathetic pride in his conquests, and gloried in his power. At one time, under the ancient monarchy, the French felt a sort of satisfaction in the sense of their dependence upon the arbitrary pleasure of their king, and they were wont to say with pride, "We are the subjects of the most powerful king in the world."

But, like all instinctive passions, this kind of patriotism is more apt to prompt transient exertion than to supply the motives of continuous endeavor. It may save the state in critical circumstances, but it will not unfrequently allow the nation to decline in the midst of peace. Whilst the manners of a people are simple and its faith unshaken, whilst society is steadily based upon traditional institutions whose legitimacy has never been contested, this instinctive patriotism is wont to endure.

But there is another species of attachment to a country which is more rational than the one we have been describing. It is perhaps less generous and less ardent, but it is more fruitful and more lasting; it is coeval with the spread of knowledge, it is nurtured by the laws, it grows by the exercise of civil rights, and, in the end, it is confounded with the personal interest of the citizen. A man comprehends the influence which the prosperity of his country has upon his own welfare; he is aware that the laws authorize him to contribute his assistance to that prosperity, and he labors to promote it as a portion of his interest in the first place, and as a portion of his right in the second. . . .

In the United States the inhabitants were thrown but as yesterday upon the soil which they now occupy, and they brought neither customs nor traditions with them there; they meet each other for the first time with no previous acquaintance; in short, the instinctive love of their country can scarcely exist in their minds; but everyone takes as zealous an interest in the affairs of his township, his county, and of the whole state, as if they were his own, because everyone, in his sphere, takes an active part in the government of society.

The lower orders in the United States are alive to the perception of the influence exercised by the general prosperity upon their own welfare; and simple as this observation is, it is one which is but too rarely made by the people. But in America the people regards this prosperity as the result of its own exertions; the citizen looks upon the fortune of the public as his private interest, and he co-operates in its success, not so much from a sense of pride or of duty, as from what I shall venture to term cupidity.

It is unnecessary to study the institutions and the history of the Americans in order to discover the truth of this remark, for their manners render it sufficiently evident. As the American participates in all that is done in his country, he thinks himself obliged to defend whatever may be censured; for it is not only his country which is attacked upon these occasions, but it is himself. The consequence is, that his national pride resorts to a thousand artifices, and to all the petty tricks of individual vanity.

Nothing is more embarrassing in the ordinary intercourse of life than this irritable patriotism of the Americans. A stranger may be very well inclined to praise many of the institutions of their country, but he begs permission to blame some of the peculiarities which he observes—a permission which is, however, inexorably refused. America is therefore a free country, in which, lest anybody should be hurt by your remarks, you are not allowed to speak freely of private individuals, or of the state, of the citizens or of the authorities, of public or of private undertakings, or, in short, of anything at all, except it be of the climate and the soil; and even then Americans will be found ready to defend either the one or the other, as if they had been contrived by the inhabitants of the country.

After the idea of virtue, I know no higher principle than that of right; or, to speak more accurately, these two ideas are commingled in one. The idea of right is simply that of virtue introduced into the political world. It is the idea of right which enabled men to define anarchy and tyranny; and which taught them to remain independent without arrogance, as well as to obey without servility. The man who submits to violence is debased by his compliance; but when he obeys the mandate of one who possesses that right of authority which he acknowledges in a fellow-creature, he rises in some measure above the person who delivers the command. There are no great men without virtue, and there are no great nations—it may almost be added that there would be no society—without the notion of rights; for what is the condition of a mass of rational and intelligent beings who are only united together by the bond of force?

I am persuaded that the only means which we possess at the present time of inculcating the notion of rights, and of rendering it, as it were, palpable to the senses, is to invest all the members of the community with the peaceful exercise of certain rights: this is very clearly seen in children, who are men without the strength and the experience of manhood. When a child begins to move in the midst of the objects which surround him, he is instinctively led to turn everything which he can lay his hands upon to his own purposes; he has no notion of the property of others; but as he gradually learns the value of things, and begins to per-

ceive that he may in his turn be deprived of his possessions, he becomes more circumspect, and he observes
those rights in others which he wishes to have respected
in himself. The principle which the child derives from
the possession of his toys is taught to the man by the
objects which he may call his own. In America those
complaints against property in general which are so frequent in Europe are never heard, because in America
there are no paupers; and as everyone has property of
his own to defend, everyone recognizes the principle
upon which he holds it.

The same thing occurs in the political world. In
America the lowest classes have conceived a very high
notion of political rights, because they exercise those
rights; and they refrain from attacking those of other
people, in order to ensure their own from attack.
Whilst in Europe the same classes sometimes recalci-
trate even against the supreme power, the American
submits without a murmur to the authority of the pet-
tiest magistrate. . . .

The government of democracy brings the notion of
political rights to the level of the humblest citizens, just
as the dissemination of wealth brings the notion of
property within the reach of all the members of the
community; and I confess that, to my mind, this is one
of its greatest advantages. I do not assert that it is easy
to teach men to exercise political rights; but I maintain

that, when it is possible, the effects which result from it are highly important; and I add that, if there ever was a time at which such an attempt ought to be made, that time is our own. It is clear that the influence of religious belief is shaken, and that the notion of divine rights is declining; it is evident that public morality is vitiated, and the notion of moral rights is also disappearing: these are general symptoms of the substitution of argument for faith, and of calculation for the impulses of sentiment. If, in the midst of this general disruption, you do not succeed in connecting the notion of rights with that of personal interest, which is the only immutable point in the human heart, what means will you have of governing the world except by fear? When I am told that, since the laws are weak and the populace is wild, since passions are excited and the authority of virtue is paralyzed, no measures must be taken to increase the rights of the democracy, I reply, that it is for these very reasons that some measures of the kind must be taken; and I am persuaded that governments are still more interested in taking them than society at large, because governments are liable to be destroyed and society cannot perish.

I am not, however, inclined to exaggerate the example which America furnishes. In those states the people are invested with political rights at a time when they could scarcely be abused, for the citizens were few in number and simple in their manners. As they have increased, the Americans have not augmented the power of the democracy, but they have, if I may use the expression, extended its dominions. It cannot be doubted that the moment at which political rights are granted to a people that had before been without them is a very critical, though it be a necessary one. A child may kill before he is aware of the value of life; and he may deprive another person of his property before he is aware that his own may be taken away from him. The lower orders, when first they are invested with political rights, stand, in relation to those rights, in the same position as the child does to the whole of nature, and the celebrated adage may then be applied to them, Homo puer robustus. This truth may even be perceived in America. The states in which the citizens have enjoyed their rights longest are those in which they make the best use of them.

It cannot be repeated too often that nothing is more fertile in prodigies than the art of being free; but there is nothing more arduous than the apprenticeship of liberty. Such is not the case with despotic institutions: despotism often promises to make amends for a thousand previous ills; it supports the right, it protects the oppressed, and it maintains public order. The nation is lulled by the temporary prosperity which accrues to it, until it is roused to a sense of its own misery. Liberty, on the contrary, is generally established in the midst of agitation, it is perfected by civil discord, and its benefits cannot be appreciated until it is already old. . . .

It is not always feasible to consult the whole people, either directly or indirectly, in the formation of the law; but it cannot be denied that, when such a measure is possible the authority of the law is very much augmented. This popular origin, which impairs the excellence and the wisdom of legislation, contributes prodigiously to increase its power. There is an amazing strength in the expression of the determination of a whole people, and when it declares itself the imagination of those who are most inclined to contest it is overawed by its authority. The truth of this fact is very well known by parties, and they consequently strive to make out a majority whenever they can. If they have not the greater number of voters on their side, they assert that the true majority abstained from voting; and if they are foiled even there, they have recourse to the body of those persons who had no votes to give.

In the United States, except slaves, servants, and paupers in the receipt of relief from the townships, there is no class of persons who do not exercise the elective franchise, and who do not indirectly contribute to make the laws. Those who design to attack the laws must consequently either modify the opinion of the nation or trample upon its decision.

A second reason, which is still more weighty, may be further adduced; in the United States everyone is personally interested in enforcing the obedience of the whole community to the law; for as the minority may shortly rally the majority to its principles, it is interested in professing that respect for the decrees of the legislator which it may soon have occasion to claim for its own. However irksome an enactment may be, the citizen of the United States complies with it, not only because it is the work of the majority, but because it originates in his own authority, and he regards it as a contract to which he is himself a party.

In the United States, then, that numerous and turbulent multitude does not exist which always looks upon the law as its natural enemy, and accordingly surveys it with fear and with fear and with distrust. It is impossible, on the other hand, not to perceive that all classes display the utmost reliance upon the legislation of their country, and that they are attached to it by a kind of parental affection.

I am wrong, however, in saying all classes; for as in America the European scale of authority is inverted, the wealthy are there placed in a position analogous to that of the poor in the Old World, and it is the opulent classes which frequently look upon the law with suspicion. I have already observed that the advantage of democracy is not, as has been sometimes asserted, that it protects the interests of the whole community, but simply that it protects those of the majority. In the United States, where the poor rule, the rich have always some reason to dread the abuses of their power. This natural anxiety of the rich may produce a sullen dissatisfaction, but society is not disturbed by it; for the same reason which induces the rich to withhold their confidence in the legislative authority makes them obey its mandates; their wealth, which prevents them from making the law, prevents them from withstanding it. Amongst civilized nations revolts are rarely excited, except by such persons as have nothing to lose by them; and if the laws of a democracy are not always worthy of respect, at least they always obtain it; for those who usually infringe the laws have no excuse for not complying with the enactments they have themselves made, and by which they are themselves benefited, whilst the citizens whose interests might be promoted by the infraction of them are induced, by their character and their stations, to submit to the decisions of the legislature, whatever they may be. Besides which, the people in America obeys the law not only because it emanates from the popular authority, but because that authority may modify it in any points which may prove vexatory; a law is observed because it is a self-imposed evil in the first place, and an evil of transient duration in the second. . . .

It is not impossible to conceive the surpassing liberty which the Americans enjoy; some idea may likewise be formed of the extreme equality which subsists amongst them, but the political activity which pervades the United States must be seen in order to be understood. No sooner do you set foot upon the American soil than you are stunned by a kind of tumult; a confused clamor is heard on every side; and a thousand simultaneous voices demand the immediate satisfaction of their social wants. Everything is in motion around you; here, the people of one quarter of a town are met to decide upon the building of a church; there, the election of a representative is going on; a little further the delegates of a district are posting to the town in order to consult upon some local improvements; or in another place the laborers of a village quit their ploughs to deliberate upon the project of a road or a public school. Meetings are called for the sole purpose of declaring their disapprobation of the line of conduct pursued by the government; whilst in other assemblies the citizens salute the authorities of the day as the fathers of their country. Societies are formed which regard drunkenness as the principal cause of the evils under which the state labors, and which solemnly bind themselves to give a constant example of temperance.

The great political agitation of the American legislative bodies, which is the only kind of excitement that attracts the attention of foreign countries, is a mere episode or a sort of continuation of that universal movement which originates in the lowest classes of the people and extends successively to all the ranks of society. It is impossible to spend more efforts in the pursuit of enjoyment.

The cares of political life engross a most prominent place in the occupation of a citizen in the United States, and almost the only pleasure of which an American has any idea is to take a part in the government, and to discuss the part he has taken. This feeling pervades the most trifling habits of life; even the women frequently attend public meetings and listen to political harangues as a recreation after their household labors. Debating clubs are to a certain extent a substitute for theatrical entertainments: an American cannot converse, but he can discuss; and when he attempts to talk he falls into a dissertation. He speaks to you as if he was addressing a meeting; and if he should chance to warm in the course of the discussion, he will infallibly say, "Gentlemen," to the person with whom he is conversing. . . .

This ceaseless agitation which democratic government has introduced into the political world influences all social intercourse. I am not sure that upon the whole this is not the greatest advantage of democracy. And I

am much less inclined to applaud it for what it does
than for what it causes to be done. It is incontestable
that the people frequently conducts public business
very ill; but it is impossible that the lower orders should
take a part in public business without extending the
circle of their ideas, and without quitting the ordinary
routine of their mental acquirements. The humblest
individual who is called upon to co-operate in the government of society acquires a certain degree of self-
respect; and as he possesses authority, he can command
the services of minds much more enlightened than his
own. He is canvassed by a multitude of applicants, who
seek to deceive him in a thousand different ways, but
who instruct him by their deceit. He takes a part in
political undertakings which did not originate in his
own conception, but which give him a taste for undertakings of the kind. New ameliorations are daily
pointed out in the property which he holds in common
with others, and this gives him the desire of improving
that property which is more peculiarly his own. He is
perhaps neither happier nor better than those who came
before him, but he is better informed and more active. I
have no doubt that the democratic institutions of the
United States, joined to the physical constitution of the
country, are the cause (not the direct, as is so often
asserted, but the indirect cause) of the prodigious commercial activity of the inhabitants. It is not engendered

by the laws, but the people learns how to promote it by the experience derived from legislation.

When the opponents of democracy assert that a single individual performs the duties which he undertakes much better than the government of the community, it appears to me that they are perfectly right. The government of an individual, supposing an equality of instruction on either side, is more consistent, more persevering, and more accurate than that of a multitude, and it is much better qualified judiciously to discriminate the characters of the men it employs. If any deny what I advance, they have certainly never seen a democratic government, or have formed their opinion upon very partial evidence. It is true that even when local circumstances and the disposition of the people allow democratic institutions to subsist, they never display a regular and methodical system of government. Democratic liberty is far from accomplishing all the projects it undertakes, with the skill of an adroit despotism. It frequently abandons them before they have borne their fruits, or risks them when the consequences may prove dangerous; but in the end it produces more than any absolute government, and if it do fewer things well, it does a greater number of things. Under its sway the transactions of the public administration are not nearly so important as what is done by private exertion. Democracy does not confer the most skilful kind of

government upon the people, but it produces that which
the most skilful governments are frequently unable to
awaken, namely, an all-pervading and restless activity, a
superabundant force, and an energy which is insepara-
ble from it, and which may, under favorable circumstances, beget the most amazing benefits. These are the
true advantages of democracy. . . .

Chapter VII

UNLIMITED POWER OF MAJORITY,

AND ITS CONSEQUENCES

The very essence of democratic government consists in
the absolute sovereignty of the majority; for there is
nothing in democratic states which is capable of resisting it. Most of the American Constitutions have sought
to increase this natural strength of the majority by arti-
ficial means.

The legislature is, of all political institutions, the
one which is most easily swayed by the wishes of the
majority. The Americans determined that the members
of the legislature should be elected by the people immediately, and for a very brief term, in order to subject
them, not only to the general convictions, but even to
the daily passion, of their constituents. The members of
both houses are taken from the same class in society,
and are nominated in the same manner; so that the
modifications of the legislative bodies are almost as

rapid and quite as irresistible as those of a single assembly. It is to a legislature thus constituted that almost all the authority of the government has been entrusted.

But whilst the law increased the strength of those authorities which of themselves were strong, it enfeebled more and more those which were naturally weak. It deprived the representatives of the executive of all stability and independence, and by subjecting them completely to the caprices of the legislature, it robbed them of the slender influence which the nature of a democratic government might have allowed them to retain. In several states the judicial power was also submitted to the elective discretion of the majority, and in all of them its existence was made to depend on the pleasure of the legislative authority, since the representatives were empowered annually to regulate the stipend of the judges.

Custom, however, has done even more than law. A proceeding which will in the end set all the guarantees of representative government at naught is becoming more and more general in the United States; it frequently happens that the electors, who choose a delegate, point out a certain line of conduct to him, and impose upon him a certain number of positive obligations which he is pledged to fulfil. With the exception of the tumult, this comes to the same thing as if the majority of the populace held its deliberations in the market-place.

Several other circumstances concur in rendering the power of the majority in America not only preponderant, but irresistible. The moral authority of the majority is partly based upon the notion that there is more intelligence and more wisdom in a great number of men collected together than in a single individual, and that the quantity of legislators is more important than their quality. The theory of equality is in fact applied to the intellect of man: and human pride is thus assailed in its last retreat by a doctrine which the minority hesitate to admit, and in which they very slowly concur. Like all other powers, and perhaps more than all other powers, the authority of the many requires the sanction of time; at first it enforces obedience by constraint, but its laws are not respected until they have long been maintained.

The right of governing society, which the majority supposes itself to derive from its superior intelligence, was introduced into the United States by the first settlers, and this idea, which would be sufficient of itself to create a free nation, has now been amalgamated with the manners of the people and the minor incidents of social intercourse.

The French, under the old monarchy, held it for a maxim (which is still a fundamental principle of the English Constitution) that the King could do no wrong; and if he did do wrong, the blame was imputed to his advisers. This notion was highly favorable to habits of obedience, and it enabled the subject to complain of the law without ceasing to love and honor the lawgiver. The Americans entertain the same opinion with respect to the majority.

The moral power of the majority is founded upon yet another principle, which is, that the interests of the many are to be preferred to those of the few. It will readily be perceived that the respect here professed for the rights of the majority must naturally increase or diminish according to the state of parties. When a nation is divided into several irreconcilable factions, the privilege of the majority is often overlooked, because it is intolerable to comply with its demands. . . .

There are certain communities in which the persons who constitute the minority can never hope to draw over the majority to their side, because they must then give up the very point which is at issue between them. Thus, an aristocracy can never become a majority whilst it retains its exclusive privileges, and it cannot cede its privileges without ceasing to be an aristocracy.

In the United States political questions cannot be taken up in so general and absolute a manner, and all parties are willing to recognize the right of the majority, because they all hope to turn those rights to their own advantage at some future time. The majority therefore in that country exercises a prodigious actual authority, and a moral influence which is scarcely less preponderant; no obstacles exist which can impede or so much as retard its progress, or which can induce it to heed the complaints of those whom it crushes upon its path. This state of things is fatal in itself and dangerous for the future.

I have already spoken of the natural defects of democratic institutions, and they all of them increase at the exact ratio of the power of the majority. To begin with the most evident of them all; the mutability of the laws is an evil inherent in democratic government, because it is natural to democracies to raise men to power in very rapid succession. But this evil is more or less sensible in proportion to the authority and the means of action which the legislature possesses.

In America the authority exercised by the legislative bodies is supreme; nothing prevents them from accomplishing their wishes with celerity, and with irresistible power, whilst they are supplied by new representatives every year. That is to say, the circumstances which contribute most powerfully to democratic instability, and which admit of the free application of caprice to every object in the state, are here in full operation. In conformity with this principle, America is, at the present day, the country in the world where laws last the shortest time. Almost all the American constitutions have been amended within the course of thirty years: there is therefore not a single American state which has not modified the principles of its legislation in that lapse of time. As for the laws themselves, a single glance upon the archives of the different states of the union suffices to convince one that in America the activity of the legislator never slackens. Not that the American democracy is naturally less stable than any other, but that it is allowed to follow its capricious propensities in the formation of the laws.

The omnipotence of the majority, and the rapid as well as absolute manner in which its decisions are executed in the United States, has not only the effect of rendering the law unstable, but it exercises the same influence upon the execution of the law and the conduct of the public administration. As the majority is the only power which it is important to court, all its projects are taken up with the greatest ardor, but no sooner is its attention distracted than all this ardor ceases; whilst in the free states of Europe the administration is at once independent and secure, so that the projects of the legislature are put into execution, although its immediate attention may be directed to other objects.

In America certain ameliorations are undertaken with much more zeal and activity than elsewhere; in Europe the same ends are promoted by much less social effort, more continuously applied.

Some years ago several pious individuals undertook to ameliorate the condition of the prisons. The public was excited by the statements which they put forward, and the regeneration of criminals became a very popular undertaking. New prisons were built, and for the first time the idea of reforming as well as of punishing the delinquent formed a part of prison discipline. But this happy alteration, in which the public had taken so hearty an interest, and which the exertions of the citizens had irresistibly accelerated, could not be completed in a moment. Whilst the new penitentiaries were being erected (and it was the pleasure of the majority that they should be terminated with all possible celerity), the old prisons existed, which still contained a great number of offenders. These jails became more unwholesome and more corrupt in proportion as the new establishments were beautified and improved, forming a contrast which may readily be understood. The majority was so eagerly employed in founding the new prisons that those which already existed were forgotten; and as the general attention was diverted to a novel object, the care which had hitherto been bestowed upon the others ceased. The salutary regulations of discipline were first relaxed, and afterwards broken; so that in the immediate neighborhood of a prison which bore witness to the mild and enlightened spirit of our time, dungeons might be met with which reminded the visitor of the barbarity of the Middle Ages. . . .

Tyranny of the Majority

I hold it to be an impious and an execrable maxim that, politically speaking, a people has a right to do whatsoever it pleases, and yet I have asserted that all authority originates in the will of the majority. Am I then, in contradiction with myself?

A general law—which bears the name of Justice— has been made and sanctioned, not only by a majority of this or that people, but by a majority of mankind. The rights of every people are consequently confined within the limits of what is just. A nation may be considered in the light of a jury which is empowered to represent society at large, and to apply the great and general law of justice. Ought such a jury, which represents society, to have more power than the society in which the laws it applies originate?

When I refuse to obey an unjust law, I do not contest the right which the majority has of commanding, but I simply appeal from the sovereignty of the people to the sovereignty of mankind. It has been asserted that a people can never entirely outstep the boundaries of justice and of reason in those affairs which are more peculiarly its own, and that consequently, full power may fearlessly be given to the majority by which it is represented. But this language is that of a slave.

A majority taken collectively may be regarded as a being whose opinions, and most frequently whose interests, are opposed to those of another being, which is styled a minority. If it be admitted that a man, possessing absolute power, may misuse that power by wronging his adversaries, why should a majority not be liable to the same reproach? Men are not apt to change their characters by agglomeration; nor does their patience in the presence of obstacles increase with the consciousness of their strength. And for these reasons I can never willingly invest any number of my fellow-creatures with that unlimited authority which I should refuse to any one of them.

I do not think that it is possible to combine several principles in the same government, so as at the same time to maintain freedom, and really to oppose them to one another. The form of government which is usually termed mixed has always appeared to me to be a mere chimera. Accurately speaking there is no such thing as a mixed government (with the meaning usually given to that word), because in all communities some one principle of action may be discovered which preponderates over the others. England in the last century, which has been more especially cited as an example of this form of government, was in point of fact an essentially aristo-

cratic state, although it comprised very powerful elements of democracy; for the laws and customs of the
country were such that the aristocracy could not but
preponderate in the end, and subject the direction of
public affairs to its own will. The error arose from too
much attention being paid to the actual struggle which
was going on between the nobles and the people, without considering the probable issue of the contest, which
was in reality the important point. When a community
really has a mixed government, that is to say, when it is
equally divided between two adverse principles, it must
either pass through a revolution or fall into complete
dissolution.

I am therefore of opinion that some one social
power must always be made to predominate over the
others; but I think that liberty is endangered when this
power is checked by no obstacles which may retard its
course, and force it to moderate its own vehemence.

Unlimited power is in itself a bad and dangerous
thing; human beings are not competent to exercise it
with discretion, and God alone can be omnipotent,
because His wisdom and His justice are always equal to
His power. But no power upon earth is so worthy of
honor for itself, or of reverential obedience to the rights
which it represents, that I would consent to admit its
uncontrolled and all-predominant authority. When I
see that the right and the means of absolute command

are conferred on a people or upon a king, upon an aristocracy or a democracy, a monarchy or a republic, I recognize the germ of tyranny, and I journey onward to a land of more hopeful institutions.

In my opinion the main evil of the present democratic institutions of the United States does not arise, as is often asserted in Europe, from their weakness, but from their overpowering strength; and I am not so much alarmed at the excessive liberty which reigns in that country as at the very inadequate securities which exist against tyranny.

When an individual or a party is wronged in the United States, to whom can he apply for redress? If to public opinion, public opinion constitutes the majority; if to the legislature, it represents the majority, and implicitly obeys its injunctions; if to the executive power, it is appointed by the majority, and remains a passive tool in its hands; the public troops consist of the majority under arms; the jury is the majority invested with the right of hearing judicial cases; and in certain states even the judges are elected by the majority. However iniquitous or absurd the evil of which you complain may be, you must submit to it as well as you can.

If, on the other hand, a legislative power could be so constituted as to represent the majority without necessarily being the slave of its passions; an executive, so as to retain a certain degree of uncontrolled authority; and a judiciary, so as to remain independent of the two other powers; a government would be formed which would still be democratic without incurring any risk of tyrannical abuse.

I do not say that tyrannical abuses frequently occur in America at the present day, but I maintain that no sure barrier is established against them, and that the causes which mitigate the government are to be found in the circumstances and the manners of the country more than in its laws.

A distinction must be drawn between tyranny and arbitrary power. Tyranny may be exercised by means of the law, and in that case it is not arbitrary; arbitrary power may be exercised for the good of the community at large, in which case it is not tyrannical. Tyranny usually employs arbitrary means, but, if necessary, it can rule without them. . . .

It is in the examination of the display of public opinion in the United States that we clearly perceive how far the power of the majority surpasses all the powers with which we are acquainted in Europe. Intellectual principles exercise an influence which is so invisible, and often so inappreciable, that they baffle the toils of oppression. At the present time the most absolute monarchs in Europe are unable to prevent certain notions, which are opposed to their authority, from circulating in secret throughout their dominions, and even in their courts. Such is not the case in America; as long as the majority is still undecided, discussion is carried on; but as soon as its decision is irrevocably pronounced, a submissive silence is observed, and the friends, as well as the opponents, of the measure unite in assenting to its propriety. The reason of this is perfectly clear: no monarch is so absolute as to combine all the powers of society in his own hands, and to conquer all opposition with the energy of a majority which is invested with the right of making and of executing the laws. . . .

In America the majority raises very formidable barriers to the liberty of opinion: within these barriers an author may write whatever he pleases, but he will repent it if he ever step beyond them. Not that he is exposed to the terrors of an auto-da-fe, but he is tormented by the slights and persecutions of daily obloquy. His political career is closed forever, since he has offended the only authority which is able to promote his success. Every sort of compensation, even that of celebrity, is refused to him. Before he published his opinions he imagined that he held them in common with many others; but no sooner has he declared them openly than he is loudly censured by his overbearing opponents, whilst those who think without having the courage to speak, like him, abandon him in silence. He yields at length, oppressed by the daily efforts he has been making, and he subsides into silence, as if he was tormented by remorse for having spoken the truth.

Fetters and headsmen were the coarse instruments which tyranny formerly employed; but the civilization of our age has refined the arts of despotism which seemed, however, to have been sufficiently perfected before. The excesses of monarchical power had devised a variety of physical means of oppression: the democratic republics of the present day have rendered it as entirely an affair of the mind as that will which it is intended to coerce. Under the absolute sway of an individual despot the body was attacked in order to subdue the soul, and the soul escaped the blows which were directed against it and rose superior to the attempt; but such is not the course adopted by tyranny in democratic republics; there the body is left free, and the soul is enslaved. The sovereign can no longer say, "You shall think as I do on pain of death"; but he says, "You are free to think differently from me, and to retain your life, your property, and all that you possess; but if such be your determination, you are henceforth an alien among your people. You may retain your civil rights, but they will be useless to you, for you will never be chosen by your fellow-citizens if you solicit their suffrages, and they will affect to scorn you if you solicit their esteem. You will remain among men, but you will be deprived of the rights of mankind. Your fellow-creatures will shun you like an impure being, and those who are most persuaded of your innocence will abandon you too, lest they should be shunned in their turn. Go in peace! I have given you your life, but it is an existence in comparably worse than death." . . .

The tendencies which I have just alluded to are as yet very slightly perceptible in political society, but they already begin to exercise an unfavorable influence upon the national character of the Americans. I am inclined to attribute the singular paucity of distinguished political characters to the ever-increasing activity of the despotism of the majority in the United States. When the American Revolution broke out they arose in great numbers, for public opinion then served, not to tyrannize over, but to direct the exertions of individuals. Those celebrated men took a full part in the general agitation of mind common at that period, and they attained a high degree of personal fame, which was reflected back upon the nation, but which was by no means borrowed from it. . . .

In free countries, where everyone is more or less called upon to give his opinion in the affairs of state; in democratic republics, where public life is incessantly commingled with domestic affairs, where the sovereign authority is accessible on every side, and where its attention can almost always be attracted by vociferation, more persons are to be met with who speculate upon its

foibles and live at the cost of its passions than in absolute monarchies. Not because men are naturally worse
in these states than elsewhere, but the temptation is
stronger, and of easier access at the same time. The
result is a far more extensive debasement of the characters of citizens.

Democratic republics extend the practice of currying
favor with the many, and they introduce it into a greater
number of classes at once: this is one of the most serious
reproaches that can be addressed to them. In democratic
states organized on the principles of the American
republics, this is more especially the case, where the
authority of the majority is so absolute and so irresistible
that a man must give up his rights as a citizen, and
almost abjure his quality as a human being, if he intends
to stray from the track which it lays down. . . .

If ever these lines are read in America, I am well
assured of two things: in the first place, that all who
peruse them will raise their voices to condemn me; and
in the second place, that very many of them will acquit
me at the bottom of their conscience. . . .

Governments usually fall a sacrifice to impotence
or to tyranny. In the former case their power escapes
from them; it is wrested from their grasp in the latter.
Many observers, who have witnessed the anarchy of
democratic states, have imagined that the government
of those states was naturally weak and impotent. The

truth is, that when once hostilities are begun between parties, the government loses its control over society. But I do not think that a democratic power is naturally without force or without resources: say, rather, that it is almost always by the abuse of its force and the misemployment of its resources that a democratic government fails. Anarchy is almost always produced by its tyranny or its mistakes, but not by its want of strength.

It is important not to confound stability with force, or the greatness of a thing with its duration. In democratic republics, the power which directs society is not stable; for it often changes hands and assumes a new direction. But whichever way it turns, its force is almost irresistible. The governments of the American republics appear to me to be as much centralized as those of the absolute monarchies of Europe, and more energetic than they are. I do not, therefore, imagine that they will perish from weakness.

If ever the free institutions of America are destroyed, that event may be attributed to the unlimited authority of the majority, which may at some future time urge the minorities to desperation, and oblige them to have recourse to physical force. Anarchy will then be the result, but it will have been brought about by despotism. . . .

Chapter VIII

CAUSES MITIGATING TYRANNY IN THE UNITED STATES

I have already pointed out the distinction which is to be made between a centralized government and a centralized administration. The former exists in America, but the latter is nearly unknown there. If the directing power of the American communities had both these instruments of government at its disposal, and united the habit of executing its own commands to the right of commanding; if, after having established the general principles of government, it descended to the details of public business; and if, having regulated the great interests of the country, it could penetrate into the privacy of individual interests, freedom would soon be banished from the New World.

But in the United States the majority, which so frequently displays the tastes and the propensities of a despot, is still destitute of the more perfect instruments of tyranny. In the American republics the activity of the central government has never as yet been extended beyond a limited number of objects sufficiently prominent to call forth its attention. The secondary affairs of society have never been regulated by its authority, and nothing has hitherto betrayed its desire of interfering in them. The majority is become more and more absolute, but it has not increased the prerogatives of the central government; those great prerogatives have been confined to a certain sphere; and although the despotism of the majority may be galling upon one point, it cannot be said to extend to all. However the predominant party in the nation may be carried away by its passions, however ardent it may be in the pursuit of its projects, it cannot oblige all the citizens to comply with its desires in the same manner and at the same time throughout the country. When the central government which represents that majority has issued a decree, it must entrust the execution of its will to agents, over whom it frequently has no control, and whom it cannot perpetually direct. The townships, municipal bodies, and counties may therefore be looked upon as concealed breakwaters, which check or part the tide of popular excitement. If an oppressive law were passed, the liberties of the people would still be protected by the means by which that law would be put in execution: the majority cannot descend to the details and (as I will venture to style them) the puerilities of administrative tyranny. Nor does the people entertain that full consciousness of its authority which would prompt it to interfere in these matters; it knows the extent of its natural powers, but it is unacquainted with the increased resources which the art of government might furnish.

This point deserves attention, for if a democratic

republic similar to that of the United States were ever founded in a country where the power of a single individual had previously subsisted, and the effects of a centralized administration had sunk deep into the habits and the laws of the people, I do not hesitate to assert, that in that country a more insufferable despotism would prevail than any which now exists in the monarchical states of Europe, or indeed than any which could be found on this side of the confines of Asia.

In visiting the Americans and in studying their laws we perceive that the authority they have entrusted to members of the legal profession, and the influence which these individuals exercise in the government, is the most powerful existing security against the excesses of democracy. This effect seems to me to result from a general cause which it is useful to investigate, since it may produce analogous consequences elsewhere.

The members of the legal profession have taken an important part in all the vicissitudes of political society in Europe during the last five hundred years. At one time they have been the instruments of those who were invested with political authority, and at another they have succeeded in converting political authorities into their instrument. In the Middle Ages they afforded a powerful support to the Crown, and since that period they have exerted themselves to the utmost to limit the royal prerogative. In England they have contracted a close alliance with the aristocracy; in France they have proved to be the most dangerous enemies of that class. It is my object to inquire whether, under all these circumstances, the members of the legal profession have been swayed by sudden and momentary impulses; or whether they have been impelled by principles which are inherent in their pursuits, and which will always recur in history. I am incited to this investigation by reflecting that this particular class of men will most likely play a prominent part in that order of things to which the events of our time are giving birth.

Men who have more especially devoted themselves to legal pursuits derive from those occupations certain habits of order, a taste for formalities, and a kind of instinctive regard for the regular connection of ideas, which naturally render them very hostile to the revolutionary spirit and the unreflecting passions of the multitude.

The special information which lawyers derive from their studies ensures them a separate station in society, and they constitute a sort of privileged body in the scale of intelligence. This notion of their superiority perpetually recurs to them in the practice of their profession: they are the masters of a science which is necessary, but which is not very generally known; they serve as arbiters between the citizens; and the habit of directing the blind passions of parties in litigation to their purpose inspires them with a certain contempt for the judgment of the multitude. To this it may be added that they naturally constitute a body, not by any previous understanding, or by an agreement which directs them to a common end; but the analogy of their studies and the uniformity of their proceedings connect their minds together, as much as a common interest could combine their endeavors.

A portion of the tastes and of the habits of the aristocracy may consequently be discovered in the characters of men in the profession of the law. They participate in the same instinctive love of order and of formalities; and they entertain the same repugnance to the actions of the multitude, and the same secret contempt of the government of the people. I do not mean to say that the natural propensities of lawyers are sufficiently strong to sway them irresistibly; for they, like most other men, are governed by their private interests and the advantages of the moment.

In a state of society in which the members of the legal profession are prevented from holding that rank in the political world which they enjoy in private life, we may rest assured that they will be the foremost agents of revolution. But it must then be inquired whether the cause which induces them to innovate and to destroy is accidental, or whether it belongs to some lasting purpose which they entertain. It is true that lawyers mainly contributed to the overthrow of the French monarchy in 1789; but it remains to be seen whether they acted thus because they had studied the laws, or because they were prohibited from co-operating in the work of legislation. . . .

I do not, then, assert that all the members of the legal profession are at all times the friends of order and the opponents of innovation, but merely that most of them usually are so. In a community in which lawyers are allowed to occupy, without opposition, that high station which naturally belongs to them, their general spirit will be eminently conservative and anti-democratic. When an aristocracy excludes the leaders of that profession from its ranks, it excites enemies which are the more formidable to its security as they are independent of the nobility by their industrious pursuits; and they feel themselves to be its equal in point of intelligence, although they enjoy less opulence and less power. But whenever an aristocracy consents to impart some of its privileges to these same individuals, the two classes coalesce very readily, and assume, as it were, the consistency of a single order of family interests. . . .

Lawyers are attached to public order beyond every other consideration, and the best security of public order is authority. It must not be forgotten that, if they prize the free institutions of their country much, they nevertheless value the legality of those institutions far more: they are less afraid of tyranny than of arbitrary power; and provided that the legislature take upon itself to deprive men of their independence, they are not dissatisfied. . . .

The government of democracy is favorable to the political power of lawyers; for when the wealthy, the noble, and the prince are excluded from the government, they are sure to occupy the highest stations, in their own right, as it were, since they are the only men of information and sagacity, beyond the sphere of the people, who can be the object of the popular choice. If, then, they are led by their tastes to combine with the aristocracy and to support the Crown, they are naturally brought into contact with the people by their interests. They like the government of democracy, without participating in its propensities and without imitating its weaknesses; whence they derive a twofold authority, from it and over it. The people in democratic states does not mistrust the members of the legal profession, because it is well known that they are interested in serving the popular cause; and it listens to them without irritation, because it does not attribute to them any sinister designs. The object of lawyers is not, indeed, to overthrow the institutions of democracy, but they constantly endeavor to give it an impulse which diverts it from its real tendency, by means which are foreign to its nature. Lawyers belong to the people by birth and interest, to the aristocracy by habit and by taste, and they may be looked upon as the natural bond and connecting link of the two great classes of society.

The profession of the law is the only aristocratic element which can be amalgamated without violence with the natural elements of democracy, and which can be advantageously and permanently combined with them. I am not unacquainted with the defects which are inherent in the character of that body of men; but without this admixture of lawyer-like sobriety with the democratic principle, I question whether democratic institutions could long be maintained, and I cannot believe that a republic could subsist at the present time if the influence of lawyers in public business did not increase in proportion to the power of the people.

This aristocratic character, which I hold to be common to the legal profession, is much more distinctly marked in the United States and in England than in any other country. This proceeds not only from the legal studies of the English and American lawyers, but from the nature of the legislation, and the position which those persons occupy in the two countries. The English and the Americans have retained the law of precedents; that is to say, they continue to found their legal opinions and the decisions of their courts upon the opinions and the decisions of their forefathers. In the mind of an

English or American lawyer a taste and a reverence for what is old is almost always united to a love of regular and lawful proceedings. . . .

In America there are no nobles or men of letters, and the people is apt to mistrust the wealthy; lawyers consequently form the highest political class, and the most cultivated circle of society. They have therefore nothing to gain by innovation, which adds a conservative interest to their natural taste for public order. If I were asked where I place the American aristocracy, I should reply without hesitation that it is not composed of the rich, who are united together by no common tie, but that it occupies the judicial bench and the bar.

The more we reflect upon all that occurs in the United States the more shall we be persuaded that the lawyers as a body form the most powerful, if not the only, counterpoise to the democratic element. In that country we perceive how eminently the legal profession is qualified by its powers, and even by its defects, to neutralize the vices which are inherent in popular government. When the American people is intoxicated by passion, or carried away by the impetuosity of its ideas, it is checked and stopped by the almost invisible influence of its legal counsellors, who secretly oppose their aristocratic propensities to its democratic instincts, their superstitious attachment to what is antique to its love of novelty, their narrow views to its immense designs, and their habitual procrastination to its ardent impatience.

The courts of justice are the most visible organs by which the legal profession is enabled to control the democracy. The judge is a lawyer, who, independently of the taste for regularity and order which he has contracted in the study of legislation, derives an additional love of stability from his own inalienable functions. His legal attainments have already raised him to a distinguished rank amongst his fellow-citizens; his political power completes the distinction of his station, and gives him the inclinations natural to privileged classes.

Armed with the power of declaring the laws to be unconstitutional, the American magistrate perpetually interferes in political affairs. He cannot force the people to make laws, but at least he can oblige it not to disobey its own enactments; or to act inconsistently with its own principles. I am aware that a secret tendency to diminish the judicial power exists in the United States, and by most of the constitutions of the several states the government can, upon the demand of the two houses of the legislature, remove the judges from their station. By some other constitutions the members of the tribunals are elected, and they are even subjected to frequent re-elections. I venture to predict that these innovations will sooner or later be attended with fatal consequences, and that it will be found out at some future period that the attack which is made upon the judicial power has affected the democratic republic itself.

It must not, however, be supposed that the legal spirit of which I have been speaking has been confined, in the United States, to the courts of justice; it extends far beyond them. As the lawyers constitute the only enlightened class which the people does not mistrust, they are naturally called upon to occupy most of the public stations. They fill the legislative assemblies, and they conduct the administration; they consequently exercise a powerful influence upon the formation of the law, and upon its execution. The lawyers are, however, obliged to yield to the current of public opinion, which is too strong for them to resist it, but it is easy to find indications of what their conduct would be if they were free to act as they chose. The Americans, who have made such copious innovations in their political legislation, have introduced very sparing alterations in their civil laws, and that with great difficulty, although those laws are frequently repugnant to their social condition. The reason of this is, that in matters of civil law the majority is obliged to defer to the authority of the legal profession, and that the American lawyers are disinclined to innovate when they are left to their own choice. . . .

Chapter X

FUTURE CONDITION OF THREE RACES

IN THE UNITED STATES

The principal part of the task which I had imposed upon myself is now performed. I have shown, as far as I was able, the laws and the manners of the American democracy. Here I might stop; but the reader would perhaps feel that I had not satisfied his expectations.

The absolute supremacy of democracy is not all that we meet with in America; the inhabitants of the New World may be considered from more than one point of view. In the course of this work my subject has often led me to speak of the Indians and the Negroes; but I have never been able to stop in order to show what place these two races occupy in the midst of the democratic people whom I was engaged in describing. I have mentioned in what spirit, and according to what laws, the Anglo-American union was formed; but I could only glance at the dangers which menace that confederation, whilst it was equally impossible for me to give a detailed account of its chances of duration, independently of its laws and manners. When speaking of the united republican states, I hazarded no conjectures upon the permanence of republican forms in the New World, and when making frequent allusion to the commercial activity which reigns in the union, I was unable to inquire into the future condition of the Americans as a commercial people.

These topics are collaterally connected with my subject without forming a part of it; they are American without being democratic; and to portray democracy has been my principal aim. It was therefore necessary to postpone these questions, which I now take up as the proper termination of my work.

The territory now occupied or claimed by the American union spreads from the shores of the Atlantic to those of the Pacific Ocean. On the east and west its limits are those of the continent itself. On the south it advances nearly to the tropic, and it extends upwards to the icy regions of the north. The human beings who are scattered over this space do not form, as in Europe, so many branches of the same stock. Three races, naturally distinct, and, I might almost say, hostile to each other, are discoverable amongst them at the first glance. Almost insurmountable barriers had been raised between them by education and by law, as well as by their origin and outward characteristics; but fortune has brought them together on the same soil, where, although they are mixed, they do not amalgamate, and each race fulfils its destiny apart.

Amongst these widely differing families of men, the first which attracts attention, the superior in intelligence, in power and in enjoyment, is the white or European, the man pre-eminent; and in subordinate grades, the negro and the Indian. These two unhappy races have nothing in common; neither birth, nor features, nor language, nor habits. Their only resemblance lies in their misfortunes. Both of them occupy an inferior rank in the country they inhabit; both suffer from tyranny; and if their wrongs are not the same, they originate, at any rate, with the same authors.

If we reasoned from what passes in the world, we should almost say that the European is to the other races of mankind, what man is to the lower animals;—he makes them subservient to his use; and when he cannot subdue, he destroys them. Oppression has, at one stroke, deprived the descendants of the Africans of almost all the privileges of humanity. The negro of the United States has lost all remembrance of his country; the language which his forefathers spoke is never heard around him; he abjured their religion and forgot their customs when he ceased to belong to Africa, without acquiring any claim to European privileges. But he remains half way between the two communities; sold by the one, repulsed by the other; finding not a spot in the universe to call by the name of country, except the faint image of a home which the shelter of his master's roof affords.

The negro has no family; woman is merely the temporary companion of his pleasures, and his children are upon an equality with himself from the moment of their birth. Am I to call it a proof of God's mercy or a visitation of his wrath, that man in certain states appears to be insensible to his extreme wretchedness, and almost affects, with a depraved taste, the cause of his misfortunes? The negro, who is plunged in this abyss of evils, scarcely feels his own calamitous situation. Violence made him a slave, and the habit of servitude gives him the thoughts and desires of a slave; he admires his tyrants more than he hates them, and finds his joy and his pride in the servile imitation of those who oppress him: his understanding is degraded to the level of his soul.

The negro enters upon slavery as soon as he is born: nay, he may have been purchased in the womb, and have begun his slavery before he began his existence. Equally devoid of wants and of enjoyment, and useless to himself, he learns, with his first notions of existence, that he is the property of another, who has an interest in preserving his life, and that the care of it does not devolve upon himself; even the power of thought appears to him a useless gift of Providence, and he quietly enjoys the privileges of his debasement. If he becomes free, independence is often felt by him to be a heavier burden than slavery; for having learned, in the course of his life, to submit to everything except reason, he is too much unacquainted with her dictates to obey them. A thousand new desires beset him, and he is destitute of the knowledge and energy necessary to resist them: these are masters which it is necessary to contend with, and he has learnt only to submit and obey. In short, he sinks to such a depth of wretchedness, that while servitude brutalizes, liberty destroys him.

Oppression has been no less fatal to the Indian than to the negro race, but its effects are different. Before the arrival of white men in the New World, the inhabitants of North America lived quietly in their woods, enduring the vicissitudes and practising the virtues and vices common to savage nations. The Europeans, having dispersed the Indian tribes and driven them into the deserts, condemned them to a wandering life full of inexpressible sufferings.

Savage nations are only controlled by opinion and by custom. When the North American Indians had lost the sentiment of attachment to their country; when their families were dispersed, their traditions obscured, and the chain of their recollections broken; when all their habits were changed, and their wants increased beyond measure, European tyranny rendered them more disorderly and less civilized than they were before. The moral and physical condition of these tribes continually grew worse, and they became more barbarous as they became more wretched. Nevertheless, the Europeans have not been able to metamorphose the character of the Indians; and though they have had power to destroy them, they have never been able to make them submit to the rules of civilized society.

The lot of the negro is placed on the extreme limit of servitude, while that of the Indian lies on the uttermost verge of liberty; and slavery does not produce more fatal effects upon the first, than independence upon the second. The negro has lost all property in his own person, and he cannot dispose of his existence without committing a sort of fraud: but the savage is his own master as soon as he is able to act; parental authority is scarcely known to him; he has never bent his will to that of any of his kind, nor learned the difference between voluntary obedience and a shameful subjection; and the very name of law is unknown to him. To be free, with him, signifies to escape from all the shackles of society. As he delights in this barbarous independence, and would rather perish than sacrifice the least part of it, civilization has little power over him.

The negro makes a thousand fruitless efforts to insinuate himself amongst men who repulse him; he conforms to the tastes of his oppressors, adopts their opinions, and hopes by imitating them to form a part of their community. Having been told from infancy that his race is naturally inferior to that of the whites, he assents to the proposition and is ashamed of his own nature. In each of his features he discovers a trace of slavery, and, if it were in his power, he would willingly rid himself of everything that makes him what he is.

The Indian, on the contrary, has his imagination inflated with the pretended nobility of his origin, and lives and dies in the midst of these dreams of pride. Far from desiring to conform his habits to ours, he loves his savage life as the distinguishing mark of his race, and he repels every advance to civilization, less perhaps from the hatred which he entertains for it, than from a dread of resembling the Europeans. While he has nothing to oppose to our perfection in the arts but the resources of the desert, to our tactics nothing but undisciplined courage; whilst our well-digested plans are met by the spontaneous instincts of savage life, who can wonder if he fails in this unequal contest?

The negro, who earnestly desires to mingle his race with that of the European, cannot effect it; while the Indian, who might succeed to a certain extent, disdains to make the attempt. The servility of the one dooms him to slavery, the pride of the other to death. . . .

None of the Indian tribes which formerly inhabited the territory of New England—the Naragansetts, the Mohicans, the Pecots—have any existence but in the recollection of man. The Lenapes, who received William Penn, a hundred and fifty years ago, upon the banks of the Delaware, have disappeared; and I myself met with the last of the Iroquois, who were begging alms. The nations I have mentioned formerly covered the country to the sea-coast; but a traveller at the present day must penetrate more than a hundred leagues into the interior of the continent to find an Indian. Not only have these wild tribes receded, but they are destroyed; and as they give way or perish, an immense and increasing people fills their place. There is no instance upon record of so prodigious a growth, or so rapid a destruction: the manner in which the latter change takes place is not difficult to describe. . . .

The Indians will not live as Europeans live, and yet they can neither subsist without them, nor exactly after the fashion of their fathers.

From the moment when a European settlement is formed in the neighborhood of the territory occupied by the Indians, the beasts of chase take the alarm. . . .

A few European families, settled in different situations at a considerable distance from each other, soon drive away the wild animals which remain between their places of abode. The Indians, who had previously lived in a sort of abundance, then find it difficult to subsist, and still more difficult to procure the articles of barter which they stand in need of.

To drive away their game is to deprive them of the means of existence, as effectually as if the fields of our agriculturists were stricken with barrenness; and they are reduced, like famished wolves, to prowl through the forsaken woods in quest of prey. Their instinctive love of their country attaches them to the soil which gave them birth, even after it has ceased to yield anything but misery and death. At length they are compelled to acquiesce, and to depart: they follow the traces of the elk, the buffalo, and the beaver, and are guided by these wild animals in the choice of their future country. Properly speaking, therefore, it is not the Europeans who drive away the native inhabitants of America; it is famine which compels them to recede; a happy distinction which had escaped the casuists of former times, and for which we are indebted to modern discovery!

It is impossible to conceive the extent of the sufferings which attend these forced emigrations. They are undertaken by a people already exhausted and reduced; and the countries to which the newcomers betake themselves are inhabited by other tribes which receive them with jealous hostility. Hunger is in the rear; war awaits them, and misery besets them on all sides. . . .

These are great evils; and it must be added that they appear to me to be irremediable. I believe that the Indian nations of North America are doomed to perish; and that whenever the Europeans shall be established on the shores of the Pacific Ocean, that race of men will be no more. The Indians had only the two alternatives of war or civilization; in other words, they must either have destroyed the Europeans or become their equals.

At the first settlement of the colonies they might have found it possible, by uniting their forces, to deliver themselves from the small bodies of strangers who landed on their continent. They several times attempted to do it, and were on the point of succeeding; but the disproportion of their resources, at the present day, when compared with those of the whites, is too great to allow such an enterprise to be thought of. Nevertheless, there do arise from time to time among the Indians men of penetration, who foresee the final destiny which awaits the native population, and who exert themselves to unite all the tribes in common hostility to the Europeans; but their efforts are unavailing. Those tribes which are in the neighborhood of the whites, are too much weakened to offer an effectual resistance; whilst the others, giving way to that childish carelessness of the morrow which characterizes savage life, wait for the near approach of danger before they prepare to meet it; some are unable, the others are unwilling, to exert themselves.

It is easy to foresee that the Indians will never conform to civilization; or that it will be too late, whenever they may be inclined to make the experiment. . . .

. . . From whichever side we consider the destinies of the aborigines of North America, their calamities appear to be irremediable: if they continue barbarous, they are forced to retire; if they attempt to civilize their

manners, the contact of a more civilized community
subjects them to oppression and destitution. They perish if they continue to wander from waste to waste, and
if they attempt to settle they still must perish; the assistance of Europeans is necessary to instruct them, but
the approach of Europeans corrupts and repels them
into savage life; they refuse to change their habits as
long as their solitudes are their own, and it is too late to
change them when they are constrained to submit. . . .

The Indians will perish in the same isolated condition in which they have lived; but the destiny of the
negroes is in some measure interwoven with that of the
Europeans. These two races are attached to each other
without intermingling, and they are alike unable entirely
to separate or to combine. The most formidable of all
the ills which threaten the future existence of the union
arises from the presence of a black population upon its
territory; and in contemplating the cause of the present
embarrassments or of the future dangers of the United
States, the observer is invariably led to consider this as
a primary fact.

The permanent evils to which mankind is subjected
are usually produced by the vehement or the increasing
efforts of men; but there is one calamity which penetrated furtively into the world, and which was at first
scarcely distinguishable amidst the ordinary abuses of
power; it originated with an individual whose name his-

tory has not preserved; it was wafted like some accursed germ upon a portion of the soil, but it afterwards nurtured itself, grew without effort, and spreads naturally with the society to which it belongs. I need scarcely add that this calamity is slavery. Christianity suppressed slavery, but the Christians of the sixteenth century re-established it—as an exception, indeed, to their social system, and restricted to one of the races of mankind; but the wound thus inflicted upon humanity, though less extensive, was at the same time rendered far more difficult of cure.

It is important to make an accurate distinction between slavery itself and its consequences. The immediate evils which are produced by slavery were very nearly the same in antiquity as they are amongst the moderns; but the consequences of these evils were different. The slave, amongst the ancients, belonged to the same race as his master, and he was often the superior of the two in education and instruction. Freedom was the only distinction between them; and when freedom was conferred they were easily confounded together. The ancients, then, had a very simple means of avoiding slavery and its evil consequences, which was that of affranchisement; and they succeeded as soon as they adopted this measure generally. Not but, in ancient states, the vestiges of servitude subsisted for some time after servitude itself was abolished. There is a natural prejudice which prompts men to despise whomsoever has been their inferior long after he is become their equal; and the real inequality which is produced by fortune or by law is always succeeded by an imaginary inequality which is implanted in the manners of the people. Nevertheless, this secondary consequence of slavery was limited to a certain term amongst the ancients, for the freedman bore so entire a resemblance to those born free, that it soon became impossible to distinguish him from amongst them.

The greatest difficulty in antiquity was that of altering the law; amongst the moderns it is that of altering the manners; and, as far as we are concerned, the real obstacles begin where those of the ancients left off. This arises from the circumstance that, amongst the moderns, the abstract and transient fact of slavery is fatally united to the physical and permanent fact of color. The tradition of slavery dishonors the race, and the peculiarity of the race perpetuates the tradition of slavery. No African has ever voluntarily emigrated to the shores of the New World; whence it must be inferred, that all the blacks who are now to be found in that hemisphere are either slaves or freedmen. Thus the negro transmits the eternal mark of his ignominy to all his descendants; and although the law may abolish slavery, God alone can obliterate the traces of its existence.

The modern slave differs from his master not only

in his condition, but in his origin. You may set the negro free, but you cannot make him otherwise than an alien to the European. Nor is this all; we scarcely acknowledge the common features of mankind in this child of debasement whom slavery has brought amongst us. His physiognomy is to our eyes hideous, his understanding weak, his tastes low; and we are almost inclined to look upon him as a being intermediate between man and the brutes. The moderns, then, after they have abolished slavery, have three prejudices to contend against, which are less easy to attack and far less easy to conquer than the mere fact of servitude: the prejudice of the master, the prejudice of the race, and the prejudice of color.

It is difficult for us, who have had the good fortune to be born amongst men like ourselves by nature, and equal to ourselves by law, to conceive the irreconcilable differences which separate the negro from the European in America. But we may derive some faint notion of them from analogy. France was formerly a country in which numerous distinctions of rank existed, that had been created by the legislation. Nothing can be more fictitious than a purely legal inferiority; nothing more contrary to the instinct of mankind than these permanent divisions which had been established between beings evidently similar. Nevertheless these divisions subsisted for ages; they still subsist in many

places; and on all sides they have left imaginary vestiges, which time alone can efface. If it be so difficult
to root out an inequality which solely originates in the
law, how are those distinctions to be destroyed which
seem to be based upon the immutable laws of nature
herself? When I remember the extreme difficulty with
which aristocratic bodies, of whatever nature they may
be, are commingled with the mass of the people; and
the exceeding care which they take to preserve the
ideal boundaries of their caste inviolate, I despair of
seeing an aristocracy disappear which is founded upon
visible and indelible signs. Those who hope that the
Europeans will ever mix with the negroes, appear to
me to delude themselves; and I am not led to any such
conclusion by my own reason, or by the evidence of
facts. . . .

I see that in a certain portion of the territory of the
United States at the present day, the legal barrier which
separated the two races is tending to fall away, but not
that which exists in the manners of the country; slavery
recedes, but the prejudice to which it has given birth
remains stationary. Whosoever has inhabited the
United States must have perceived that in those parts of
the union in which the negroes are no longer slaves, they
have in no wise drawn nearer to the whites. On the contrary, the prejudice of the race appears to be stronger in
the states which have abolished slavery, than in those

where it still exists; and nowhere is it so intolerant as in those states where servitude has never been known.

It is true, that in the north of the union, marriages may be legally contracted between negroes and whites; but public opinion would stigmatize a man who should connect himself with a negress as infamous, and it would be difficult to meet with a single instance of such a union. The electoral franchise has been conferred upon the negroes in almost all the states in which slavery has been abolished; but if they come forward to vote, their lives are in danger. If oppressed, they may bring an action at law, but they will find none but whites amongst their judges; and although they may legally serve as jurors, prejudice repulses them from that office. The same schools do not receive the child of the black and of the European. In the theatres, gold cannot procure a seat for the servile race beside their former masters; in the hospitals they lie apart; and although they are allowed to invoke the same Divinity as the whites, it must be at a different altar, and in their own churches, with their own clergy. The gates of heaven are not closed against these unhappy beings; but their inferiority is continued to the very confines of the other world; when the negro is defunct, his bones are cast aside, and the distinction of condition prevails even in the equality of death. The negro is free, but he can share neither the rights, nor the pleasures, nor the labor, nor the afflictions, nor the tomb of him whose equal he has been declared to be; and he cannot meet him upon fair terms in life or in death.

In the south, where slavery still exists, the negroes are less carefully kept apart; they sometimes share the labor and the recreations of the whites; the whites consent to intermix with them to a certain extent, and although the legislation treats them more harshly, the habits of the people are more tolerant and compassionate. In the South the master is not afraid to raise his slave to his own standing, because he knows that he can in a moment reduce him to the dust at pleasure. In the north the white no longer distinctly perceives the barrier which separates him from the degraded race, and he shuns the negro with the more pertinacity, since he fears lest they should some day be confounded together. . . .

Thus it is, in the United States, that the prejudice which repels the negroes seems to increase in proportion as they are emancipated, and inequality is sanctioned by the manners whilst it is effaced from the laws of the country. But if the relative position of the two races which inhabit the United States is such as I have described, it may be asked why the Americans have abolished slavery in the north of the union, why they maintain it in the south, and why they aggravate its hardships there? The answer is easily given. It is not for the good of the negroes, but for that of the whites, that measures are taken to abolish slavery in the United States. . . .

A century had scarcely elapsed since the foundation of the colonies, when the attention of the planters was struck by the extraordinary fact, that the provinces which were comparatively destitute of slaves, increased in population, in wealth, and in prosperity more rapidly than those which contained the greatest number of negroes. In the former, however, the inhabitants were obliged to cultivate the soil themselves, or by hired laborers; in the latter they were furnished with hands for which they paid no wages; yet although labor and expenses were on the one side, and ease with economy on the other, the former were in possession of the most advantageous system. This consequence seemed to be the more difficult to explain, since the settlers, who all belonged to the same European race, had the same habits, the same civilization, the same laws, and their shades of difference were extremely slight.

Time, however, continued to advance, and the Anglo-Americans, spreading beyond the coasts of the Atlantic Ocean, penetrated farther and farther into the solitudes of the West; they met with a new soil and an unwonted climate; the obstacles which opposed them were of the most various character; their races intermingled, the inhabitants of the south went up towards the north, those of the north descended to the south; but in the midst of all these causes, the same result occurred at every step, and in general, the colonies in which there were no slaves became more populous and more rich than those in which slavery flourished. The more progress was made, the more was it shown that slavery, which is so cruel to the slave, is prejudicial to the master.

But this truth was most satisfactorily demonstrated when civilization reached the banks of the Ohio. The stream which the Indians had distinguished by the name of Ohio, or Beautiful River, waters one of the most magnificent valleys that has ever been made the abode of man. Undulating lands extend upon both shores of the Ohio, whose soil affords inexhaustible treasures to the laborer; on either bank the air is wholesome and the climate mild, and each of them forms the extreme frontier of a vast state: That which follows the numerous windings of the Ohio upon the left is called Kentucky, that upon the right bears the name of the river. These two states only differ in a single respect; Kentucky has admitted slavery, but the state of Ohio has prohibited the existence of slaves within its borders.

Thus the traveller who floats down the current of the Ohio to the spot where that river falls into the Mississippi, may be said to sail between liberty and servitude; and a transient inspection of the surrounding objects will convince him as to which of the two is most favorable to mankind. Upon the left bank of the stream the population is rare; from time to time one descries a troop of slaves loitering in the half-desert fields; the primaeval forest recurs at every turn; society seems to be asleep, man to be idle, and nature alone offers a scene of activity and of life. From the right bank, on the contrary, a confused hum is heard which proclaims the presence of industry; the fields are covered with abundant harvests, the elegance of the dwellings announces the taste and activity of the laborer, and man appears to be in the enjoyment of that wealth and contentment which is the reward of labor. . . .

Upon the left bank of the Ohio labor is confounded with the idea of slavery, upon the right bank it is identified with that of prosperity and improvement; on the one side it is degraded, on the other it is honored; on the former territory no white laborers can be found, for they would be afraid of assimilating themselves to the negroes; on the latter no one is idle, for the white population extends its activity and its intelligence to every kind of employment. Thus the men whose task it is to cultivate the rich soil of Kentucky are ignorant and lukewarm; whilst those who are active and enlightened either do nothing or pass over into the state of Ohio, where they may work without dishonor. . . .

The influence of slavery extends still further; it

affects the character of the master, and imparts a peculiar tendency to his ideas and his tastes. Upon both banks of the Ohio, the character of the inhabitants is enterprising and energetic; but this vigor is very differently exercised in the two states. The white inhabitant of Ohio, who is obliged to subsist by his own exertions, regards temporal prosperity as the principal aim of his existence; and as the country which he occupies presents inexhaustible resources to his industry and ever-varying lures to his activity, his acquisitive ardor surpasses the ordinary limits of human cupidity: he is tormented by the desire of wealth, and he boldly enters upon every path which fortune opens to him; he becomes a sailor, a pioneer, an artisan, or a laborer with the same indifference, and he supports, with equal constancy, the fatigues and the dangers incidental to these various professions; the resources of his intelligence are astonishing, and his avidity in the pursuit of gain amounts to a species of heroism.

But the Kentuckian scorns not only labor, but all the undertakings which labor promotes; as he lives in an idle independence, his tastes are those of an idle man; money loses a portion of its value in his eyes; he covets wealth much less than pleasure and excitement; and the energy which his neighbor devotes to gain, turns with him to a passionate love of field sports and military exercises; he delights in violent bodily exertion, he is familiar with the use of arms, and is accustomed from a very early age to expose his life in single combat. . . .

The emancipated negroes, and those born after the abolition of slavery, do not, indeed, migrate from the north to the south; but their situation with regard to the Europeans is not unlike that of the aborigines of America; they remain half civilized, and deprived of their rights in the midst of a population which is far superior to them in wealth and in knowledge; where they are exposed to the tyranny of the laws and the intolerance of the people. On some accounts they are still more to be pitied than the Indians, since they are haunted by the reminiscence of slavery, and they cannot claim possession of a single portion of the soil: many of them perish miserably, and the rest congregate in the great towns, where they perform the meanest offices, and lead a degraded existence. . . .

As long as the negro remains a slave, he may be kept in a condition not very far removed from that of the brutes; but, with his liberty, he cannot but acquire a degree of instruction which will enable him to appreciate his misfortunes, and to discern a remedy for them. Moreover, there exists a singular principle of relative justice which is very firmly implanted in the human heart. Men are much more forcibly struck by those inequalities which exist within the circle of the same

class, than with those which may be remarked between
different classes. It is more easy for them to admit slavery, than to allow several millions of citizens to exist
under a load of eternal infamy and hereditary wretchedness. In the north the population of freed negroes feels
these hardships and resents these indignities; but its
numbers and its powers are small, whilst in the south it
would be numerous and strong.

As soon as it is admitted that the whites and the
emancipated blacks are placed upon the same territory
in the situation of two alien communities, it will readily
be understood that there are but two alternatives for the
future; the negroes and the whites must either wholly
part or wholly mingle. I have already expressed the con-
viction which I entertain as to the latter event. I do not
imagine that the white and black races will ever live in
any country upon an equal footing. But I believe the
difficulty to be still greater in the United States than
elsewhere. An isolated individual may surmount the
prejudices of religion, of his country, or of his race, and
if this individual is a king he may effect surprising
changes in society; but a whole people cannot rise, as it
were, above itself. A despot who should subject the
Americans and their former slaves to the same yoke,
might perhaps succeed in commingling their races; but
as long as the American democracy remains at the head
of affairs, no one will undertake so difficult a task; and

it may be foreseen that the freer the white population of the United States becomes, the more isolated will it remain. . . .

If I were called upon to predict what will probably occur at some future time, I should say, that the abolition of slavery in the south will, in the common course of things, increase the repugnance of the white population for the men of color. I found this opinion upon the analogous observation which I already had occasion to make in the north. I there remarked that the white inhabitants of the north avoid the negroes with increasing care, in proportion as the legal barriers of separation are removed by the legislature; and why should not the same result take place in the south? In the north, the whites are deterred from intermingling with the blacks by the fear of an imaginary danger; in the south, where the danger would be real, I cannot imagine that the fear would be less general. . . .

The danger of a conflict between the white and the black inhabitants of the southern states of the union—a danger which, however remote it may be, is inevitable—perpetually haunts the imagination of the Americans. The inhabitants of the north make it a common topic of conversation, although they have no direct injury to fear from the struggle; but they vainly endeavor to devise some means of obviating the misfortunes which they foresee. In the southern states the subject is not discussed: the planter does not allude to the future in conversing with strangers; the citizen does not communicate his apprehensions to his friends; he seeks to conceal them from himself; but there is something more alarming in the tacit forebodings of the south, than in the clamorous fears of the northern States. . . .

I am obliged to confess that I do not regard the abolition of slavery as a means of warding off the struggle of the two races in the United States. The negroes may long remain slaves without complaining; but if they are once raised to the level of free men, they will soon revolt at being deprived of all their civil rights; and as they cannot become the equals of the whites, they will speedily declare themselves as enemies. In the north everything contributed to facilitate the emancipation of the slaves; and slavery was abolished, without placing the free negroes in a position which could become formidable, since their number was too small for them ever to claim the exercise of their rights. But such is not the case in the south. The question of slavery was a question of commerce and manufacture for the slave-owners in the north; for those of the south, it is a question of life and death. God forbid that I should seek to justify the principle of negro slavery, as has been done by some American writers! But I only observe that all the countries which formerly adopted that execrable principle are not equally able to abandon it at the present time.

When I contemplate the condition of the south, I can only discover two alternatives which may be adopted by the white inhabitants of those states; viz., either to emancipate the negroes, and to intermingle with them; or, remaining isolated from them, to keep them in a state of slavery as long as possible. All intermediate measures seem to me likely to terminate, and that shortly, in the most horrible of civil wars, and perhaps in the extirpation of one or other of the two races. Such is the view which the Americans of the south take of the question, and they act consistently with it. As they are determined not to mingle with the negroes, they refuse to emancipate them.

Not that the inhabitants of the south regard slavery as necessary to the wealth of the planter, for on this point many of them agree with their northern countrymen in freely admitting that slavery is prejudicial to their interest; but they are convinced that, however prejudicial it may be, they hold their lives upon no other tenure. The instruction which is now diffused in the south has convinced the inhabitants that slavery is injurious to the slave-owner, but it has also shown them, more clearly than before, that no means exist of getting rid of its bad consequences. Hence arises a singular contrast; the more the utility of slavery is contested, the more firmly is it established in the laws; and whilst the principle of servitude is gradually abolished in the north, that self-same principle gives rise to more and more rigorous consequences in the south.

The legislation of the southern states with regard to slaves, presents at the present day such unparalleled atrocities as suffice to show how radically the laws of humanity have been perverted, and to betray the desperate position of the community in which that legislation has been promulgated. The Americans of this portion of the union have not, indeed, augmented the hardships of slavery; they have, on the contrary, bettered the physical condition of the slaves. The only means by which the ancients maintained slavery were fetters and death; the Americans of the south of the union have discovered more intellectual securities for the duration of their power. They have employed their despotism and their violence against the human mind. In antiquity, precautions were taken to prevent the slave from breaking his chains; at the present day measures are adopted to deprive him even of the desire of freedom. The ancients kept the bodies of their slaves in bondage, but they placed no restraint upon the mind and no check upon education; and they acted consistently with their established principle, since a natural termination of slavery then existed, and one day or other the slave might be set free, and become the equal of his master. But the Americans of the south, who do not admit that the negroes can ever be commingled with themselves, have forbidden them to be taught to read or to write, under severe penalties; and as they will not raise them to their own level, they sink them as nearly as possible to that of the brutes. . . .

If it be impossible to anticipate a period at which the Americans of the south will mingle their blood with that of the negroes, can they allow their slaves to become free without compromising their own security? And if they are obliged to keep that race in bondage in order to save their own families, may they not be excused for availing themselves of the means best adapted to that end? The events which are taking place in the southern states of the union appear to me to be at once the most horrible and the most natural results of slavery. When I see the order of nature overthrown, and when I hear the cry of humanity in its vain struggle against the laws, my indignation does not light upon the men of our own time who are the instruments of these outrages; but I reserve my execration for those who, after a thousand years of freedom, brought back slavery into the world once more. . . .

DEMOCRACY IN AMERICA

Volume Two
Part One

Chapter V

OF THE MANNER IN WHICH RELIGION IN THE UNITED
STATES AVAILS ITSELF OF DEMOCRATIC TENDENCIES

I have laid it down in a preceding chapter that men cannot do without dogmatical belief; and even that it is very much to be desired that such belief should exist amongst them. I now add, that of all the kinds of dogmatical belief the most desirable appears to me to be dogmatical belief in matters of religion; and this is a very clear inference, even from no higher consideration than the interests of this world. There is hardly any human action, however particular a character be assigned to it, which does not originate in some very general idea men have conceived of the Deity, of his relation to mankind, of the nature of their own souls, and of their duties to their fellow-creatures. Nor can anything prevent these ideas from being the common spring from which everything else emanates. Men are therefore immeasurably interested in acquiring fixed ideas of God, of the soul, and of their common duties to their Creator and to their fellow-men; for doubt on these first principles would abandon all their actions to the impulse of chance, and would condemn them to live, to a certain extent, powerless and undisciplined.

This is then the subject on which it is most important for each of us to entertain fixed ideas; and unhappily it is also the subject on which it is most difficult for each of us, left to himself, to settle his opinions by the sole force of his reason. None but minds singularly free from the ordinary anxieties of life—minds at once penetrating, subtle, and trained by thinking—can even with the assistance of much time and care, sound the depth of these most necessary truths. And, indeed, we see that these philosophers are themselves almost always enshrouded in uncertainties; that at every step the natural light which illuminates their path grows dimmer and less secure; and that, in spite of all their efforts, they have as yet only discovered a small number of conflicting notions, on which the mind of man has been tossed about for thousands of years, without either laying a firmer grasp on truth, or finding novelty even in its errors. Studies of this nature are far above the average capacity of men; and even if the majority of mankind were capable of such pursuits, it is evident that leisure to cultivate them would still be wanting. Fixed ideas of God and human nature are indispensable to the daily practice of men's lives; but the practice of their lives prevents them from acquiring such ideas. . . .

General ideas respecting God and human nature are therefore the ideas above all others which it is most suitable to withdraw from the habitual action of private judgment, and in which there is most to gain and least to lose by recognizing a principle of authority. The first object and one of the principal advantages of religions, is to furnish to each of these fundamental questions a solution which is at once clear, precise, intelligible to the mass of mankind, and lasting. There are religions which are very false and very absurd; but it may be affirmed, that any religion which remains within the circle I have just traced, without aspiring to go beyond it (as many religions have attempted to do, for the purpose of enclosing on every side the free progress of the human mind), imposes a salutary restraint on the intellect; and it must be admitted that, if it do not save men in another world, such religion is at least very conducive to their happiness and their greatness in this. This is more especially true of men living in free countries. When the religion of a people is destroyed, doubt gets hold of the highest portions of the intellect, and half paralyzes all the rest of its powers. Every man accustoms himself to entertain none but confused and changing notions on the subjects most interesting to his fellow-creatures and himself. His opinions are ill-defended and easily abandoned: and, despairing of ever resolving by himself the hardest problems of the destiny of man, he ignobly submits to think no more about them. Such a condition cannot but enervate the soul, relax the springs of the will, and prepare a people for servitude. Nor does it only happen, in such a case, that they allow their freedom to be wrested from them; they frequently themselves surrender it. When there is no longer any principle of authority in religion any more than in politics, men are speedily frightened at the aspect of this unbounded independence. The constant agitation of all surrounding things alarms and exhausts them. As everything is at sea in the sphere of the intellect, they determine at least that the mechanism of society should be firm and fixed; and as they cannot resume their ancient belief, they assume a master.

For my own part, I doubt whether man can ever support at the same time complete religious independence and entire public freedom. And I am inclined to think, that if faith be wanting in him, he must serve; and if he be free, he must believe.

Perhaps, however, this great utility of religions is still more obvious amongst nations where equality of conditions prevails than amongst others. It must be acknowledged that equality, which brings great benefits into the world, nevertheless suggests to men (as will be shown hereafter) some very dangerous propensities. It tends to isolate them from each other, to concentrate every man's attention upon himself; and it lays open the soul to an inordinate love of material gratification. The greatest advantage of religion is to inspire diametrically contrary principles. There is no religion which does not place the object of man's desires above and beyond the treasures of earth, and which does not naturally raise his soul to regions far above those of the senses. Nor is there any which does not impose on man some sort of duties to his kind, and thus draws him at times from the contemplation of himself. This occurs in religions the most false and dangerous. Religious nations are therefore naturally strong on the very point on which democratic nations are weak; which shows of what importance it is for men to preserve their religion as their conditions become more equal. . . .

But in continuation of this branch of the subject, I find that in order for religions to maintain their authority, humanly speaking, in democratic ages, they must not only confine themselves strictly within the circle of spiritual matters: their power also depends very much on the nature of the belief they inculcate, on the external forms they assume, and on the obligations they impose. The preceding observation, that equality leads men to very general and very extensive notions, is principally to be understood as applied to the question of religion. Men living in a similar and equal condition in the world readily conceive the idea of the one God, governing every man by the same laws, and granting to every man future happiness on the same conditions. The idea of the unity of mankind constantly leads them back to the idea of the unity of the Creator; whilst, on the contrary, in a state of society where men are broken up into very unequal ranks, they are apt to devise as many deities as there are nations, castes, classes, or families, and to trace a thousand private roads to heaven. . . .

Another truth is no less clear—that religions ought to assume fewer external observances in democratic periods than at any others. In speaking of philosophical method among the Americans, I have shown that nothing is more repugnant to the human mind in an age of equality than the idea of subjection to forms. Men living at such times are impatient of figures; to their eyes symbols appear to be the puerile artifice which is used to conceal or to set off truths, which should more naturally be bared to the light of open day: they are unmoved by ceremonial observances, and they are predisposed to attach a secondary importance to the details of public worship. Those whose care it is to regulate the external forms of religion in a democratic age should pay a close attention to these natural propensities of the human mind, in order not unnecessarily to run counter to them. I firmly believe in the necessity of forms, which fix the human mind in the contemplation of abstract truths, and stimulate its ardor in the pursuit of them, whilst they invigorate its powers of retaining them steadfastly. Nor do I suppose that it is possible to maintain a religion without external observances; but, on the other hand, I am persuaded that, in the ages upon which we are entering, it would be peculiarly dangerous to multiply them beyond measure; and that they ought rather to be limited to as much as is absolutely necessary to perpetuate the doctrine itself, which is the substance of religions of which the ritual is only the form. A religion which should become more minute, more peremptory, and more surcharged with small observances at a time in which men are becoming more equal, would soon find itself reduced to a band of fanatical zealots in the midst of an infidel people.

I anticipate the objection, that as all religions have general and eternal truths for their object, they cannot thus shape themselves to the shifting spirit of every age without forfeiting their claim to certainty in the eyes of mankind. To this I reply again, that the principal opinions which constitute belief, and which theologians call articles of faith, must be very carefully distinguished from the accessories connected with them. Religions are obliged to hold fast to the former, whatever be the peculiar spirit of the age; but they should take good care not to bind themselves in the same manner to the latter at a time when everything is in transition, and when the mind, accustomed to the moving pageant of human affairs, reluctantly endures the attempt to fix it to any given point. The fixity of external and secondary things can only afford a chance of duration when civil society is itself fixed; under any other circumstances I hold it to be perilous.

We shall have occasion to see that, of all the passions which originate in, or are fostered by, equality, there is one which it renders peculiarly intense, and which it infuses at the same time into the heart of every man: I mean the love of well-being. The taste for well-being is the prominent and indelible feature of democratic ages. It may be believed that a religion which should undertake to destroy so deep seated a passion, would meet its own destruction thence in the end; and if it attempted to wean men entirely from the contemplation of the good things of this world, in order to devote their faculties exclusively to the thought of another, it may be foreseen that the soul would at length escape from its grasp, to plunge into the exclusive enjoyment of present and material pleasures. The chief concern of religions is to purify, to regulate, and to restrain the excessive and exclusive taste for well-being which men feel at periods of equality; but they would err in attempting to control it completely or to eradicate it. They will not succeed in curing men of the love of riches: but they may still persuade men to enrich themselves by none but honest means.

This brings me to a final consideration, which comprises, as it were, all the others. The more the conditions of men are equalized and assimilated to each other, the more important is it for religions, whilst they carefully abstain from the daily turmoil of secular affairs, not needlessly to run counter to the ideas which generally prevail, and the permanent interests which exist in the mass of the people. For as public opinion grows to be more and more evidently the first and most irresistible of existing powers, the religious principle has no external support strong enough to enable it long to resist its attacks. This is not less true of a democratic people, ruled by a despot, than in a republic. In ages of equality, kings may often command obedience, but the majority always commands belief: to the majority, therefore, deference is to be paid in whatsoever is not contrary to the faith. . . .

Another remark is applicable to the clergy of every communion. The American ministers of the gospel do not attempt to draw or to fix all the thoughts of man upon the life to come; they are willing to surrender a portion of his heart to the cares of the present; seeming to consider the goods of this world as important, although as secondary, objects. If they take no part themselves in productive labor, they are at least interested in its progression, and ready to applaud its results; and whilst they never cease to point to the other world as the great object of the hopes and fears of the believer, they do not forbid him honestly to court prosperity in this. Far from attempting to show that these things are distinct and contrary to one another, they study rather to find out on what point they are most nearly and closely connected. . . .

Chapter VI

OF THE PROGRESS OF ROMAN CATHOLICISM

IN THE UNITED STATES

America is the most democratic country in the world, and it is at the same time (according to reports worthy of belief) the country in which the Roman Catholic religion makes most progress. At first sight this is surprising. Two things must here be accurately distinguished: equality inclines men to wish to form their own opinions; but, on the other hand, it imbues them with the taste and the idea of unity, simplicity, and impartiality in the power which governs society. Men living in democratic ages are therefore very prone to shake off all religious authority; but if they consent to subject themselves to any authority of this kind, they choose at least that it should be single and uniform. Religious powers not radiating from a common centre are naturally repugnant to their minds; and they almost as readily conceive that there should be no religion, as that there should be several. At the present time, more than in any preceding one, Roman Catholics are seen

to lapse into infidelity, and Protestants to be converted
to Roman Catholicism. If the Roman Catholic faith be
considered within the pale of the church, it would seem
to be losing ground; without that pale, to be gaining it.
Nor is this circumstance difficult of explanation. The
men of our days are naturally disposed to believe; but,
as soon as they have any religion, they immediately find
in themselves a latent propensity which urges them
unconsciously towards Catholicism. Many of the doctrines and the practices of the Romish Church astonish
them; but they feel a secret admiration for its discipline, and its great unity attracts them. If Catholicism
could at length withdraw itself from the political ani-
mosities to which it has given rise, I have hardly any
doubt but that the same spirit of the age, which appears
to be so opposed to it, would become so favorable as to
admit of its great and sudden advancement. One of the
most ordinary weaknesses of the human intellect is to
seek to reconcile contrary principles, and to purchase
peace at the expense of logic. Thus there have ever been,
and will ever be, men who, after having submitted some
portion of their religious belief to the principle of
authority, will seek to exempt several other parts of
their faith from its influence, and to keep their minds
floating at random between liberty and obedience. But
I am inclined to believe that the number of these thinkers will be less in democratic than in other ages; and

that our posterity will tend more and more to a single division into two parts—some relinquishing Christianity entirely, and others returning to the bosom of the Church of Rome.

Part Two

Chapter I

WHY DEMOCRATIC NATIONS SHOW A MORE ARDENT
AND ENDURING LOVE OF EQUALITY THAN OF LIBERTY

The first and most intense passion which is engendered by the equality of conditions is, I need hardly say, the love of that same equality. My readers will therefore not be surprised that I speak of it before all others. Everybody has remarked that in our time, and especially in France, this passion for equality is every day gaining ground in the human heart. It has been said a hundred times that our contemporaries are far more ardently and tenaciously attached to equality than to freedom; but as I do not find that the causes of the fact have been sufficiently analyzed, I shall endeavor to point them out.

It is possible to imagine an extreme point at which freedom and equality would meet and be confounded together. Let us suppose that all the members of the community take a part in the government, and that each of them has an equal right to take a part in it. As none is different from his fellows, none can exercise a tyrannical power: men will be perfectly free, because they will all be entirely equal; and they will all be perfectly equal, because they will be entirely free. To this ideal state democratic nations tend. Such is the completest form that equality can assume upon earth; but there are a thousand others which, without being equally perfect, are not less cherished by those nations.

The principle of equality may be established in civil society, without prevailing in the political world. Equal rights may exist of indulging in the same pleasures, of entering the same professions, of frequenting the same places—in a word, of living in the same manner and seeking wealth by the same means, although all men do not take an equal share in the government. A kind of equality may even be established in the political world, though there should be no political freedom there. A man may be the equal of all his countrymen save one, who is the master of all without distinction, and who selects equally from among them all the agents of his power. Several other combinations might be easily imagined, by which very great equality would be united to institutions more or less free, or even to institutions wholly without freedom. Although men cannot become absolutely equal unless they be entirely free, and consequently equality, pushed to its furthest extent, may be confounded with freedom, yet there is good reason for distinguishing the one from the other. The taste which men have for liberty, and that which they feel for equality, are, in fact, two different things; and I am not afraid to add that, amongst democratic nations, they are two unequal things.

Upon close inspection, it will be seen that there is in every age some peculiar and preponderating fact with which all others are connected; this fact almost always gives birth to some pregnant idea or some ruling passion, which attracts to itself, and bears away in its course, all the feelings and opinions of the time: it is like a great stream, towards which each of the surrounding rivulets seems to flow. Freedom has appeared in the world at different times and under various forms; it has not been exclusively bound to any social condition, and it is not confined to democracies. Freedom cannot, therefore, form the distinguishing characteristic of democratic ages. The peculiar and preponderating fact which marks those ages as its own is the equality of conditions; the ruling passion of men in those periods is the love of this equality. Ask not what singular charm the men of democratic ages find in being equal, or what special reasons they may have for clinging so tenaciously to equality rather than to the other advantages which society holds out to them: equality is the distinguishing characteristic of the age they live in; that, of itself, is enough to explain that they prefer it to all the rest. . . .

Democratic nations are at all times fond of equality, but there are certain epochs at which the passion they entertain for it swells to the height of fury. This occurs at the moment when the old social system, long menaced, completes its own destruction after a last intestine struggle, and when the barriers of rank are at length thrown down. At such times men pounce upon equality as their booty, and they cling to it as to some precious treasure which they fear to lose. The passion for equality penetrates on every side into men's hearts, expands there, and fills them entirely. Tell them not that by this blind surrender of themselves to an exclusive passion they risk their dearest interests: they are deaf. Show them not freedom escaping from their grasp, whilst they are looking another way: they are blind—or rather, they can discern but one sole object to be desired in the universe. . . .

I think that democratic communities have a natural taste for freedom: left to themselves, they will seek it, cherish it, and view any privation of it with regret. But for equality, their passion is ardent, insatiable, incessant, invincible: they call for equality in freedom; and if they cannot obtain that, they still call for equality in slavery. They will endure poverty, servitude, barbarism—but they will not endure aristocracy. This is true at all times, and especially true in our own. All men and all powers seeking to cope with this irresistible passion, will be overthrown and destroyed by it. In our age, freedom cannot be established without it, and despotism itself cannot reign without its support.

Chapter II

OF INDIVIDUALISM IN DEMOCRATIC COUNTRIES

I have shown how it is that in ages of equality every man seeks for his opinions within himself: I am now about to show how it is that, in the same ages, all his feelings are turned towards himself alone. Individualism is a novel expression, to which a novel idea has given birth. Our fathers were only acquainted with egotism. Egotism is a passionate and exaggerated love of self, which leads a man to connect everything with his own person, and to prefer himself to everything in the world. Individualism is a mature and calm feeling, which disposes each member of the community to sever himself from the mass of his fellow-creatures; and to draw apart with his family and his friends; so that, after he has thus formed a little circle of his own, he willingly leaves society at large to itself. Egotism originates in blind instinct: individualism proceeds from erroneous judgment more than from depraved feelings; it originates as much in the deficiencies of the mind as in the perversity of the heart. Egotism blights the germ of all virtue; individualism, at first, only saps the virtues of public life; but, in the long run, it attacks and destroys all others, and is at

length absorbed in downright egotism. Egotism is a vice
as old as the world, which does not belong to one form
of society more than to another: individualism is of
democratic origin, and it threatens to spread in the
same ratio as the equality of conditions.

Amongst aristocratic nations, as families remain for
centuries in the same condition, often on the same spot,
all generations become as it were contemporaneous. . . .

Amongst democratic nations new families are constantly springing up, others are constantly falling away,
and all that remain change their condition; the woof of
time is every instant broken, and the track of generations effaced. Those who went before are soon forgotten; of those who will come after no one has any idea:
the interest of man is confined to those in close propin-
quity to himself. As each class approximates to other
classes, and intermingles with them, its members
become indifferent and as strangers to one another.
Aristocracy had made a chain of all the members of the
community, from the peasant to the king: democracy
breaks that chain, and severs every link of it. As social
conditions become more equal, the number of persons
increases who, although they are neither rich enough
nor powerful enough to exercise any great influence over
their fellow-creatures, have nevertheless acquired or
retained sufficient education and fortune to satisfy their
own wants. They owe nothing to any man, they expect

nothing from any man; they acquire the habit of always considering themselves as standing alone, and they are apt to imagine that their whole destiny is in their own hands. Thus not only does democracy make every man forget his ancestors, but it hides his descendants, and separates his contemporaries from him; it throws him back forever upon himself alone, and threatens in the end to confine him entirely within the solitude of his own heart.

Chapter IV

THAT THE AMERICANS COMBAT THE EFFECTS
OF INDIVIDUALISM BY FREE INSTITUTIONS

Despotism, which is of a very timorous nature, is never more secure of continuance than when it can keep men asunder; and all its influence is commonly exerted for that purpose. No vice of the human heart is so acceptable to it as egotism: a despot easily forgives his subjects for not loving him, provided they do not love each other. He does not ask them to assist him in governing the state; it is enough that they do not aspire to govern it themselves. He stigmatizes as turbulent and unruly spirits those who would combine their exertions to promote the prosperity of the community, and, perverting the natural meaning of words, he applauds as good citizens those who have no sympathy for any but themselves. Thus the vices which despotism engenders are precisely those which equality fosters. These two things mutually and perniciously complete and assist each other. Equality places men side by side, unconnected by any common tie; despotism raises barriers to keep them asunder; the former predisposes them not to consider their fellow-creatures, the latter makes general indifference a sort of public virtue.

Despotism then, which is at all times dangerous, is more particularly to be feared in democratic ages. It is easy to see that in those same ages men stand most in need of freedom. When the members of a community are forced to attend to public affairs, they are necessarily drawn from the circle of their own interests, and snatched at times from self-observation. As soon as a man begins to treat of public affairs in public, he begins to perceive that he is not so independent of his fellow-men as he had at first imagined, and that, in order to obtain their support, he must often lend them his co-operation.

When the public is supreme, there is no man who does not feel the value of public goodwill, or who does not endeavor to court it by drawing to himself the esteem and affection of those amongst whom he is to live. Many of the passions which congeal and keep asunder human hearts, are then obliged to retire and hide below the surface. Pride must be dissembled; disdain dares not break out; egotism fears its own self.

Under a free government, as most public offices are elective, the men whose elevated minds or aspiring hopes are too closely circumscribed in private life, constantly feel that they cannot do without the population which surrounds them. Men learn at such times to think of their fellow-men from ambitious motives; and they frequently find it, in a manner, their interest to forget themselves. . . .

The Americans have combated by free institutions the tendency of equality to keep men asunder, and they have subdued it. The legislators of America did not suppose that a general representation of the whole nation would suffice to ward off a disorder at once so natural to the frame of democratic society, and so fatal: they also thought that it would be well to infuse political life into each portion of the territory, in order to multiply to an infinite extent opportunities of acting in concert for all the members of the community, and to make them constantly feel their mutual dependence on each other. The plan was a wise one. The general affairs of a country only engage the attention of leading politicians, who assemble from time to time in the same places; and as they often lose sight of each other afterwards, no lasting ties are established between them. But if the object be to have the local affairs of a district conducted by the men who reside there, the same persons are always in contact, and they are, in a manner, forced to be acquainted, and to adapt themselves to one another. . . .

. . . Local freedom, then, which leads a great number of citizens to value the affection of their neighbors and of their kindred, perpetually brings men together, and forces them to help one another, in spite of the propensities which sever them.

In the United States the more opulent citizens take great care not to stand aloof from the people; on the contrary, they constantly keep on easy terms with the lower classes: they listen to them, they speak to them every day. They know that the rich in democracies always stand in need of the poor; and that in democratic ages you attach a poor man to you more by your manner than by benefits conferred. . . .

It would be unjust to suppose that the patriotism and the zeal which every American displays for the welfare of his fellow-citizens are wholly insincere. Although private interest directs the greater part of human actions in the United States as well as elsewhere, it does not regulate them all. I must say that I have often seen Americans make great and real sacrifices to the public welfare; and I have remarked a hundred instances in which they hardly ever failed to lend faithful support to each other. The free institutions which the inhabitants of the United States possess, and the political rights of which they make so much use, remind every citizen, and in a thousand ways, that he lives in society. They every instant impress upon his mind the notion that it is the duty, as well as the interest of men, to make themselves useful to their fellow-creatures; and as he sees no particular ground of animosity to them, since he is never either their master or their slave, his heart readily leans to the side of kindness. Men attend to the interests of the public, first by necessity, afterwards by choice: what was intentional becomes an instinct; and by dint of working for the good of one's fellow citizens, the habit and the taste for serving them is at length acquired. . . .

Chapter VIII

THE AMERICANS COMBAT INDIVIDUALISM BY THE
PRINCIPLE OF INTEREST RIGHTLY UNDERSTOOD

When the world was managed by a few rich and powerful individuals, these persons loved to entertain a lofty idea of the duties of man. They were fond of professing that it is praiseworthy to forget one's self, and that good should be done without hope of reward, as it is by the Deity himself. Such were the standard opinions of that time in morals. I doubt whether men were more virtuous in aristocratic ages than in others; but they were incessantly talking of the beauties of virtue, and its utility was only studied in secret. But since the imagination takes less lofty flights and every man's thoughts are centred in himself, moralists are alarmed by this idea of self-sacrifice, and they no longer venture to present it to the human mind. They therefore content themselves with inquiring whether the personal advantage of each member of the community does not consist in working for the good of all; and when they have hit upon some point on which private interest and public interest meet and amalgamate, they are eager to bring it into notice. Observations of this kind are gradually multiplied: what was only a single remark becomes a general principle; and it is held as a truth that man serves himself in serving his fellow-creatures, and that his private interest is to do good.

I have already shown, in several parts of this work, by what means the inhabitants of the United States almost always manage to combine their own advantage with that of their fellow-citizens: my present purpose is to point out the general rule which enables them to do so. In the United States hardly anybody talks of the beauty of virtue; but they maintain that virtue is useful, and prove it every day. The American moralists do not profess that men ought to sacrifice themselves for their fellow-creatures because it is noble to make such sacrifices; but they boldly aver that such sacrifices are as necessary to him who imposes them upon himself as to him for whose sake they are made. They have found out that in their country and their age man is brought home to himself by an irresistible force; and losing all hope of stopping that force, they turn all their thoughts to the direction of it. They therefore do not deny that every man may follow his own interest; but they endeavor to prove that it is the interest of every man to be virtuous. I shall not here enter into the reasons they allege, which would divert me from my subject: suffice it to say that they have convinced their fellow-countrymen.

. . . The principle of interest rightly understood is not a lofty one, but it is clear and sure. It does not aim at mighty objects, but it attains without excessive exertion all those at which it aims. As it lies within the reach of all capacities, everyone can without difficulty apprehend and retain it. By its admirable conformity to human weaknesses, it easily obtains great dominion; nor is that dominion precarious, since the principle checks one personal interest by another, and uses, to direct the passions, the very same instrument which excites them. The principle of interest rightly understood produces no great acts of self-sacrifice, but it suggests daily small acts of self-denial. By itself it cannot suffice to make a man virtuous, but it disciplines a number of citizens in habits of regularity, temperance, moderation, foresight, self-command; and, if it does not lead men straight to virtue by the will, it gradually draws them in that direction by their habits. If the principle of interest rightly understood were to sway the whole moral world, extraordinary virtues would doubtless be more rare; but I think that gross depravity would then also be less common. The principle of interest rightly understood perhaps prevents some men from rising far above the level of mankind; but a great number of other men, who were falling far below it, are caught and restrained by it. Observe some few individuals, they are lowered by it; survey mankind, it is raised. I am not afraid to say that the principle of interest, rightly understood, appears to me the best suited of all philosophical theories to the wants of the men of our time, and that I regard it as their chief remaining security against themselves. Towards it, therefore, the minds of the moralists of our age should turn; even should they judge it to be incomplete, it must nevertheless be adopted as necessary. . . .

Chapter IX

THAT THE AMERICANS APPLY THE PRINCIPLE
OF INTEREST RIGHTLY UNDERSTOOD
TO RELIGIOUS MATTERS

If the principle of interest rightly understood had nothing but the present world in view, it would be very insufficient; for there are many sacrifices which can only find their recompense in another; and whatever ingenuity may be put forth to demonstrate the utility of virtue, it will never be an easy task to make that man live aright who has no thoughts of dying. It is therefore necessary to ascertain whether the principle of interest rightly understood is easily compatible with religious belief. The philosophers who inculcate this system of morals tell men, that to be happy in this life they must watch their own passions and steadily control their excess; that lasting happiness can only be secured by renouncing a thousand transient gratifications; and that a man must perpetually triumph over himself, in order to secure his own advantage. The founders of almost all religions have held the same language. The track they point out to man is the same, only that the goal is more remote; instead of placing in this world the reward of the sacrifices they impose, they transport it to another. Nevertheless I cannot believe that all those who practise virtue from religious motives are only actuated by the hope of a recompense. I have known zealous Christians who constantly forgot themselves, to work with greater ardor for the happiness of their fellow-men; and I have heard them declare that all they did was only to earn the blessings of a future state. I cannot but think that they deceive themselves; I respect them too much to believe them.

Christianity indeed teaches that a man must prefer his neighbor to himself, in order to gain eternal life; but Christianity also teaches that men ought to benefit their fellow-creatures for the love of God. A sublime expression! Man, searching by his intellect into the divine

conception, and seeing that order is the purpose of
God, freely combines to prosecute the great design; and
whilst he sacrifices his personal interests to this con-
summate order of all created things, expects no other
recompense than the pleasure of contemplating it. I do
not believe that interest is the sole motive of religious
men: but I believe that interest is the principal means
which religions themselves employ to govern men, and I
do not question that this way they strike into the multitude and become popular. It is not easy clearly to perceive why the principle of interest rightly understood
should keep aloof from religious opinions; and it seems
to me more easy to show why it should draw men to
them. Let it be supposed that, in order to obtain happiness in this world, a man combats his instinct on all
occasions and deliberately calculates every action of his
life; that, instead of yielding blindly to the impetuosity
of first desires, he has learned the art of resisting them,
and that he has accustomed himself to sacrifice without
an effort the pleasure of a moment to the lasting interest
of his whole life. If such a man believes in the religion
which he professes, it will cost him but little to submit
to the restrictions it may impose. Reason herself coun-
sels him to obey, and habit has prepared him to endure
them. If he should have conceived any doubts as to the
object of his hopes, still he will not easily allow himself
to be stopped by them; and he will decide that it is wise

to risk some of the advantages of this world, in order to preserve his rights to the great inheritance promised him in another. "To be mistaken in believing that the Christian religion is true," says Pascal, "is no great loss to anyone; but how dreadful to be mistaken in believing it to be false!"

The Americans do not affect a brutal indifference to a future state; they affect no puerile pride in despising perils which they hope to escape from. They therefore profess their religion without shame and without weakness; but there generally is, even in their zeal, something so indescribably tranquil, methodical, and deliberate, that it would seem as if the head, far more than the heart, brought them to the foot of the altar. The Americans not only follow their religion from interest, but they often place in this world the interest which makes them follow it. In the Middle Ages the clergy spoke of nothing but a future state; they hardly cared to prove that a sincere Christian may be a happy man here below. But the American preachers are constantly referring to the earth; and it is only with great difficulty that they can divert their attention from it. To touch their congregations, they always show them how favorable religious opinions are to freedom and public tranquillity; and it is often difficult to ascertain from their discourses whether the principal object of religion is to procure eternal felicity in the other world, or prosperity in this.

Part Three

Chapter IX

EDUCATION OF YOUNG WOMEN IN THE UNITED STATES

No free communities ever existed without morals; and, as I observed in the former part of this work, morals are the work of woman. Consequently, whatever affects the condition of women, their habits and their opinions, has great political importance in my eyes. Amongst almost all Protestant nations young women are far more the mistresses of their own actions than they are in Catholic countries. This independence is still greater in Protestant countries, like England, which have retained or acquired the right of self-government; the spirit of freedom is then infused into the domestic circle by political habits and by religious opinions. In the United States the doctrines of Protestantism are combined with great political freedom and a most democratic state of society; and nowhere are young women surrendered so early or so completely to their own guidance. Long before an American girl arrives at the age of marriage, her emancipation from maternal control begins; she has scarcely ceased to be a child when she already thinks for herself, speaks with freedom, and acts on her own impulse. The great scene of the world is constantly open to her view; far from seeking concealment, it is every day disclosed to her more completely, and she is taught to survey it with a firm and calm gaze. Thus the vices and dangers of society are early revealed to her; as she sees them clearly, she views them without illusions, and braves them without fear; for she is full of reliance on her own strength, and her reliance seems to be shared by all who are about her. An American girl scarcely ever displays that virginal bloom in the midst of young desires, or that innocent and ingenuous grace which usually attends the European woman in the transition from girlhood to youth. It is rarely that an American woman at any age displays childish timidity or ignorance. Like the young women of Europe, she seeks to please, but she knows precisely the cost of pleasing. If she does not abandon herself to evil, at least she knows that it exists; and she is remarkable rather for purity of manners than for chastity of mind. I have been frequently surprised, and almost frightened, at the singular address and happy boldness with which young women in America contrive to manage their thoughts and their language amidst all the difficulties of stimulating conversation; a philosopher would have stumbled at every step along the narrow path which they trod without accidents and without effort. It is easy indeed to perceive that, even amidst the independence of early youth, an American woman is always mistress of herself; she indulges in all permitted pleasures, without yielding herself up to any of them; and her reason never allows the reins of self-guidance to drop, though it often seems to hold them loosely. . . .

Although the Americans are a very religious people, they do not rely on religion alone to defend the virtue of woman; they seek to arm her reason also. In this they have followed the same method as in several other respects; they first make the most vigorous efforts to bring individual independence to exercise a proper control over itself, and they do not call in the aid of religion until they have reached the utmost limits of human strength. I am aware that an education of this kind is not without danger; I am sensible that it tends to invigorate the judgment at the expense of the imagination, and to make cold and virtuous women instead of affectionate wives and agreeable companions to man. Society may be more tranquil and better regulated, but domestic life has often fewer charms. These, however, are secondary evils, which may be braved for the sake of higher interests. At the stage at which we are now arrived the time for choosing is no longer within our control; a democratic education is indispensable to protect women from the dangers with which democratic institutions and manners surround them.

Chapter X

THE YOUNG WOMAN IN THE CHARACTER OF A WIFE

In America the independence of woman is irrevocably lost in the bonds of matrimony: if an unmarried woman is less constrained there than elsewhere, a wife is subjected to stricter obligations. The former makes her father's house an abode of freedom and of pleasure; the latter lives in the home of her husband as if it were a cloister. Yet these two different conditions of life are perhaps not so contrary as may be supposed, and it is natural that the American women should pass through the one to arrive at the other.

Religious peoples and trading nations entertain peculiarly serious notions of marriage: the former consider the regularity of woman's life as the best pledge and most certain sign of the purity of her morals; the latter regard it as the highest security for the order and prosperity of the household. The Americans are at the same time a puritanical people and a commercial nation: their religious opinions, as well as their trading habits, consequently lead them to require much abnegation on the part of woman, and a constant sacrifice of her pleasures to her duties which is seldom demanded of her in Europe. Thus in the United States the inexorable opinion of the public carefully circumscribes woman within the narrow circle of domestic interest and duties, and forbids her to step beyond it.

Upon her entrance into the world a young American woman finds these notions firmly established; she sees the rules which are derived from them; she is not slow to perceive that she cannot depart for an instant from the established usages of her contemporaries, without putting in jeopardy her peace of mind, her honor, nay even her social existence; and she finds the energy required for such an act of submission in the firmness of her understanding and in the virile habits which her education has given her. It may be said that she has learned by the use of her independence to surrender it without a struggle and without a murmur when the time comes for making the sacrifice. But no American woman falls into the toils of matrimony as into a snare held out to her simplicity and ignorance. She has been taught beforehand what is expected of her, and voluntarily and freely does she enter upon this engagement. She supports her new condition with courage, because she chose it. As in America paternal discipline is very relaxed and the conjugal tie very strict, a young woman does not contract the latter without considerable circumspection and apprehension. Precocious marriages are rare. Thus American women do not marry until their understandings are exercised and ripened; whereas in other countries most women generally only begin to exercise and to ripen their understandings after marriage.

I by no means suppose, however, that the great change which takes place in all the habits of women in the United States, as soon as they are married, ought solely to be attributed to the constraint of public opinion: it is frequently imposed upon themselves by the sole effort of their own will. When the time for choosing a husband is arrived, that cold and stern reasoning power which has been educated and invigorated by the free observation of the world, teaches an American woman that a spirit of levity and independence in the bonds of marriage is a constant subject of annoyance, not of pleasure; it tells her that the amusements of the girl cannot become the recreations of the wife, and that the sources of a married woman's happiness are in the home of her husband. As she clearly discerns beforehand the only road which can lead to domestic happiness, she enters upon it at once, and follows it to the end without seeking to turn back.

The same strength of purpose which the young wives of America display, in bending themselves at once and without repining to the austere duties of their new condition, is no less manifest in all the great trials of their lives. In no country in the world are private fortunes more precarious than in the United States. It is not uncommon for the same man, in the course of his life, to rise and sink again through all the grades which lead from opulence to poverty. American women support these vicissitudes with calm and unquenchable energy: it would seem that their desires contract, as easily as they expand, with their fortunes. . . .

Chapter XII

HOW THE AMERICANS UNDERSTAND
THE EQUALITY OF THE SEXES

I have shown how democracy destroys or modifies the different inequalities which originate in society; but is this all? or does it not ultimately affect that great inequality of man and woman which has seemed, up to the present day, to be eternally based in human nature? I believe that the social changes which bring nearer to the same level the father and son, the master and servant, and superiors and inferiors generally speaking, will raise woman and make her more and more the equal of man. But here, more than ever, I feel the necessity of making myself clearly understood; for there is no subject on which the coarse and lawless fancies of our age have taken a freer range.

There are people in Europe who, confounding together the different characteristics of the sexes, would make of man and woman beings not only equal but alike. They would give to both the same functions, impose on both the same duties, and grant to both the same rights; they would mix them in all things—their occupations, their pleasures, their business. It may readily be conceived, that by thus attempting to make one sex equal to the other, both are degraded; and from so preposterous a medley of the works of nature nothing could ever result but weak men and disorderly women. It is not thus that the Americans understand that species of democratic equality which may be established between the sexes. They admit, that as nature has appointed such wide differences between the physical and moral constitution of man and woman, her manifest design was to give a distinct employment to their various faculties; and they hold that improvement does not consist in making beings so dissimilar do pretty nearly the same things, but in getting each of them to fulfil their respective tasks in the best possible manner. The Americans have applied to the sexes the great principle of political economy which governs the manufactures of our age, by carefully dividing the duties of man from those of woman, in order that the great work of society may be the better carried on.

In no country has such constant care been taken as in America to trace two clearly distinct lines of action for the two sexes, and to make them keep pace one with the other, but in two pathways which are always different. American women never manage the outward concerns of the family, or conduct a business, or take a part in political life; nor are they, on the other hand, ever compelled to perform the rough labor of the fields, or to make any of those laborious exertions which demand the exertion of physical strength. No families are so poor as to form an exception to this rule. If on the one hand an American woman cannot escape from the quiet circle of domestic employments, on the other hand she is never forced to go beyond it. Hence it is that the women of America, who often exhibit a masculine strength of understanding and a manly energy, generally preserve great delicacy of personal appearance and always retain the manners of women, although they sometimes show that they have the hearts and minds of men.

Nor have the Americans ever supposed that one consequence of democratic principles is the subversion of marital power, or the confusion of the natural authorities in families. They hold that every association must have a head in order to accomplish its object, and that the natural head of the conjugal association is man. They do not therefore deny him the right of directing his partner; and they maintain, that in the smaller association of husband and wife, as well as in the great social community, the object of democracy is to regulate and legalize the powers which are necessary, not to subvert all power. This opinion is not peculiar to one sex, and contested by the other: I never observed that the women of America consider conjugal authority as a fortunate

usurpation of their rights, nor that they thought themselves degraded by submitting to it. It appeared to me,
on the contrary, that they attach a sort of pride to the
voluntary surrender of their own will, and make it their
boast to bend themselves to the yoke, not to shake it off.
Such at least is the feeling expressed by the most virtuous of their sex; the others are silent; and in the United
States it is not the practice for a guilty wife to clamor
for the rights of women, whilst she is trampling on her
holiest duties.

It has often been remarked that in Europe a certain
degree of contempt lurks even in the flattery which men
lavish upon women: although a European frequently
affects to be the slave of woman, it may be seen that he
never sincerely thinks her his equal. In the United
States men seldom compliment women, but they daily
show how much they esteem them. They constantly
display an entire confidence in the understanding of a
wife, and a profound respect for her freedom; they have
decided that her mind is just as fitted as that of a man
to discover the plain truth, and her heart as firm to
embrace it; and they have never sought to place her virtue, any more than his, under the shelter of prejudice,
ignorance, and fear. It would seem that in Europe,
where man so easily submits to the despotic sway of
women, they are nevertheless curtailed of some of the
greatest qualities of the human species, and considered

as seductive but imperfect beings; and (what may well
provoke astonishment) women ultimately look upon
themselves in the same light, and almost consider it as
a privilege that they are entitled to show themselves
futile, feeble, and timid. The women of America claim
no such privileges.

Again, it may be said that in our morals we have
reserved strange immunities to man; so that there is, as
it were, one virtue for his use, and another for the guidance of his partner; and that, according to the opinion
of the public, the very same act may be punished alter-
nately as a crime or only as a fault. The Americans
know not this iniquitous division of duties and rights;
amongst them the seducer is as much dishonored as his
victim. It is true that the Americans rarely lavish upon
women those eager attentions which are commonly paid
them in Europe; but their conduct to women always
implies that they suppose them to be virtuous and
refined; and such is the respect entertained for the moral
freedom of the sex, that in the presence of a woman the
most guarded language is used, lest her ear should be
offended by an expression. In America a young unmarried woman may, alone and without fear, undertake a
long journey.

The legislators of the United States, who have miti-
gated almost all the penalties of criminal law, still make
rape a capital offence, and no crime is visited with more

inexorable severity by public opinion. This may be accounted for; as the Americans can conceive nothing more precious than a woman's honor, and nothing which ought so much to be respected as her independence, they hold that no punishment is too severe for the man who deprives her of them against her will. In France, where the same offence is visited with far milder penalties, it is frequently difficult to get a verdict from a jury against the prisoner. Is this a consequence of contempt of decency or contempt of women? I cannot but believe that it is a contempt of one and of the other.

Thus the Americans do not think that man and woman have either the duty or the right to perform the same offices, but they show an equal regard for both their respective parts; and though their lot is different, they consider both of them as beings of equal value. They do not give to the courage of woman the same form or the same direction as to that of man; but they never doubt her courage: and if they hold that man and his partner ought not always to exercise their intellect and understanding in the same manner, they at least believe the understanding of the one to be as sound as that of the other, and her intellect to be as clear. Thus, then, whilst they have allowed the social inferiority of woman to subsist, they have done all they could to raise her morally and intellectually to the level of man; and in this respect they appear to me to have excellently understood the true principle of democratic improvement. As for myself, I do not hesitate to avow that, although the women of the United States are confined within the narrow circle of domestic life, and their situation is in some respects one of extreme dependence, I have nowhere seen woman occupying a loftier position; and if I were asked, now that I am drawing to the close of this work, in which I have spoken of so many important things done by the Americans, to what the singular prosperity and growing strength of that people ought mainly to be attributed, I should reply—to the superiority of their women.

Chapter XVII

THAT THE ASPECT OF SOCIETY IN THE UNITED STATES
IS AT ONCE EXCITED AND MONOTONOUS

It would seem that nothing can be more adapted to stimulate and to feed curiosity than the aspect of the United States. Fortunes, opinions, and laws are there in ceaseless variation: it is as if immutable nature herself were mutable, such are the changes worked upon her by the hand of man. Yet in the end the sight of this excited community becomes monotonous, and after having watched the moving pageant for a time the spectator is tired of it. Amongst aristocratic nations every man is pretty nearly stationary in his own sphere; but men are astonishingly unlike each other—their passions, their notions, their habits, and their tastes are essentially different: nothing changes but everything differs. In democracies, on the contrary, all men are alike and do things pretty nearly alike. It is true that they are subject to great and frequent vicissitudes; but as the same events of good or adverse fortune are continually recurring, the name of the actors only is changed, the piece is always the same. The aspect of American society is animated, because men and things are always changing; but it is monotonous, because all these changes are alike.

Men living in democratic ages have many passions, but most of their passions either end in the love of riches or proceed from it. The cause of this is, not that their souls are narrower, but that the importance of money is really greater at such times. When all the members of a community are independent of or indifferent to each other, the co-operation of each of them can only be obtained by paying for it: this infinitely multiplies the purposes to which wealth may be applied, and increases its value. When the reverence which belonged to what is old has vanished, birth, condition, and profession no longer distinguish men, or scarcely distinguish them at all: hardly anything but money remains to create strongly marked differences between them, and to raise some of them above the common level. The distinction originating in wealth is increased by the disappearance and diminution of all other distinctions. Amongst aristocratic nations money only reaches to a few points on the vast circle of man's desires—in democracies it seems to lead to all. The love of wealth is therefore to be traced, either as a principal or an accessory motive, at the bottom of all that the Americans do: this gives to all their passions a sort of family likeness, and soon renders the survey of them exceedingly wearisome. This perpetual recurrence of the same passion is monotonous; the peculiar methods by which this passion seeks its own gratification are no less so. . . .

Part Four

Chapter VI

WHAT SORT OF DESPOTISM DEMOCRATIC
NATIONS HAVE TO FEAR

I had remarked during my stay in the United States, that a democratic state of society, similar to that of the Americans, might offer singular facilities for the establishment of despotism; and I perceived, upon my return to Europe, how much use had already been made by most of our rulers, of the notions, the sentiments, and the wants engendered by this same social condition, for the purpose of extending the circle of their power. This led me to think that the nations of Christendom would perhaps eventually undergo some sort of oppression

like that which hung over several of the nations of the
ancient world. A more accurate examination of the subject, and five years of further meditations, have not
diminished my apprehensions, but they have changed
the object of them. No sovereign ever lived in former
ages so absolute or so powerful as to undertake to
administer by his own agency, and without the assistance of intermediate powers, all the parts of a great
empire: none ever attempted to subject all his subjects
indiscriminately to strict uniformity of regulation, and
personally to tutor and direct every member of the
community. The notion of such an undertaking never
occurred to the human mind; and if any man had conceived it, the want of information, the imperfection of
the administrative system, and above all, the natural
obstacles caused by the inequality of conditions, would
speedily have checked the execution of so vast a design.
When the Roman emperors were at the height of their
power, the different nations of the empire still preserved
manners and customs of great diversity; although they
were subject to the same monarch, most of the provinces were separately administered; they abounded in
powerful and active municipalities; and although the
whole government of the empire was centred in the
hands of the emperor alone, and he always remained,
upon occasions, the supreme arbiter in all matters, yet
the details of social life and private occupations lay for

the most part beyond his control. The emperors possessed, it is true, an immense and unchecked power, which allowed them to gratify all their whimsical tastes, and to employ for that purpose the whole strength of the State. They frequently abused that power arbitrarily to deprive their subjects of property or of life: their tyranny was extremely onerous to the few, but it did not reach the greater number; it was fixed to some few main objects, and neglected the rest; it was violent, but its range was limited.

But it would seem that if despotism were to be established amongst the democratic nations of our days, it might assume a different character; it would be more extensive and more mild; it would degrade men without tormenting them. I do not question, that in an age of instruction and equality like our own, sovereigns might more easily succeed in collecting all political power into their own hands, and might interfere more habitually and decidedly within the circle of private interests, than any sovereign of antiquity could ever do. But this same principle of equality which facilitates despotism, tempers its rigor. We have seen how the manners of society become more humane and gentle in proportion as men become more equal and alike. When no member of the community has much power or much wealth, tyranny is, as it were, without opportunities and a field of action. As all fortunes are scanty, the passions of men are naturally circumscribed—their imagination limited, their pleasures simple. This universal moderation moderates the sovereign himself, and checks within certain limits the inordinate extent of his desires.

. . . Democratic governments may become violent and even cruel at certain periods of extreme effervescence or of great danger: but these crises will be rare and brief. When I consider the petty passions of our contemporaries, the mildness of their manners, the extent of their education, the purity of their religion, the gentleness of their morality, their regular and industrious habits, and the restraint which they almost all observe in their vices no less than in their virtues, I have no fear that they will meet with tyrants in their rulers, but rather guardians. I think then that the species of oppression by which democratic nations are menaced is unlike anything which ever before existed in the world: our contemporaries will find no prototype of it in their memories. I am trying myself to choose an expression which will accurately convey the whole of the idea I have formed of it, but in vain; the old words "despotism" and "tyranny" are inappropriate: the thing itself is new; and since I cannot name it, I must attempt to define it.

. . . The first thing that strikes the observation is an innumerable multitude of men all equal and alike, incessantly endeavoring to procure the petty and paltry pleasures with which they glut their lives. Each of them, living apart, is as a stranger to the fate of all the rest—his children and his private friends constitute to him the whole of mankind; as for the rest of his fellow-citizens, he is close to them, but he sees them not—he touches them, but he feels them not; he exists but in himself and for himself alone; and if his kindred still remain to him, he may be said at any rate to have lost his country. Above this race of men stands an immense and tutelary power, which takes upon itself alone to secure their gratifications, and to watch over their fate. That power is absolute, minute, regular, provident, and mild. It would be like the authority of a parent, if, like that authority, its object was to prepare men for manhood; but it seeks on the contrary to keep them in perpetual childhood: it is well content that the people should rejoice, provided they think of nothing but rejoicing. For their happiness such a government willingly labors, but it chooses to be the sole agent and the only arbiter of that happiness: it provides for their security, foresees and supplies their necessities, facilitates their pleasures, manages their principal concerns, directs their industry, regulates the descent of property, and subdivides their inheritances—what remains, but to spare them all the care of thinking and all the trouble of living? Thus it every day renders the exercise of the free agency of man less useful and less frequent; it circumscribes the will within a narrower range, and gradually robs a man of all the uses of himself. The principle of equality has prepared men for these things: it has predisposed men to endure them, and oftentimes to look on them as benefits.

After having thus successively taken each member of the community in its powerful grasp, and fashioned them at will, the supreme power then extends its arm over the whole community. It covers the surface of society with a network of small complicated rules, minute and uniform, through which the most original minds and the most energetic characters cannot penetrate, to rise above the crowd. The will of man is not shattered, but softened, bent, and guided: men are seldom forced by it to act, but they are constantly restrained from acting: such a power does not destroy, but it prevents existence; it does not tyrannize, but it compresses, enervates, extinguishes, and stupefies a people, till each nation is reduced to be nothing better than a flock of timid and industrious animals, of which the government is the shepherd. I have always thought that servitude of the regular, quiet, and gentle kind which I have just described, might be combined more easily than is commonly believed with some of the outward forms of freedom; and that it might even establish itself under the wing of the sovereignty of the people. . . .

Chapter VII

CONTINUATION OF THE PRECEDING CHAPTERS

I believe that it is easier to establish an absolute and despotic government amongst a people in which the conditions of society are equal, than amongst any other; and I think that if such a government were once established amongst such a people, it would not only oppress men, but would eventually strip each of them of several of the highest qualities of humanity. Despotism therefore appears to me peculiarly to be dreaded in democratic ages. I should have loved freedom, I believe, at all times, but in the time in which we live I am ready to worship it. On the other hand, I am persuaded that all who shall attempt, in the ages upon which we are entering, to base freedom upon aristocratic privilege, will fail—that all who shall attempt to draw and to retain authority within a single class, will fail. At the present day no ruler is skilful or strong enough to found a despotism, by re-establishing permanent distinctions of rank amongst his subjects: no legislator is wise or powerful enough to preserve free institutions, if he does not take equality for his first principle and his watchword. All those of our contemporaries who would establish or secure the independence and the dignity of their fellowmen, must show themselves the friends of equality; and the only worthy means of showing themselves as such, is to be so: upon this depends the success of their holy enterprise. Thus the question is not how to reconstruct aristocratic society, but how to make liberty proceed out of that democratic state of society in which God has placed us.

These two truths appear to me simple, clear, and fertile in consequences; and they naturally lead me to consider what kind of free government can be established amongst a people in which social conditions are equal. It results from the very constitution of democratic nations and from their necessities, that the power of government amongst them must be more uniform, more centralized, more extensive, more searching, and more efficient than in other countries. Society at large is naturally stronger and more active, individuals more subordinate and weak; the former does more, the latter less; and this is inevitably the case. It is not therefore to be expected that the range of private independence will ever be as extensive in democratic as in aristocratic countries—nor is this to be desired; for, amongst aristocratic nations, the mass is often sacrificed to the individual, and the prosperity of the greater number to the greatness of the few. It is both necessary and desirable that the government of a democratic people should be active and powerful: and our object should not be to render it weak or indolent, but solely to prevent it from abusing its aptitude and its strength.

The circumstance which most contributed to secure the independence of private persons in aristocratic ages, was, that the supreme power did not affect to take upon itself alone the government and administration of the community; those functions were necessarily partially left to the members of the aristocracy: so that as the supreme power was always divided, it never weighed with its whole weight and in the same manner on each individual. Not only did the government not perform everything by its immediate agency; but as most of the agents who discharged its duties derived their power not from the State, but from the circumstance of their birth, they were not perpetually under its control. The government could not make or unmake them in an instant, at pleasure, nor bend them in strict uniformity to its slightest caprice—this was an additional guarantee of private independence. I readily admit that recourse cannot be had to the same means at the present time: but I discover certain democratic expedients which may be substituted for them. Instead of vesting in the government alone all the administrative powers of which corporations and nobles have been deprived, a portion of them may be entrusted to secondary public bodies, temporarily composed of private citizens: thus the liberty of private persons will be more secure, and their equality will not be diminished. . . .

Equality awakens in men several propensities extremely

dangerous to freedom, to which the attention of the legislator ought constantly to be directed. I shall only remind the reader of the most important amongst them. Men living in democratic ages do not readily comprehend the utility of forms: they feel an instinctive contempt for them—I have elsewhere shown for what reasons. Forms excite their contempt and often their hatred; as they commonly aspire to none but easy and present gratifications, they rush onwards to the object of their desires, and the slightest delay exasperates them. This same temper, carried with them into political life, renders them hostile to forms, which perpetually retard or arrest them in some of their projects. Yet this objection which the men of democracies make to forms is the very thing which renders forms so useful to freedom; for their chief merit is to serve as a barrier between the strong and the weak, the ruler and the people, to retard the one, and give the other time to look about him. Forms become more necessary in proportion as the government becomes more active and more powerful, whilst private persons are becoming more indolent and more feeble. Thus democratic nations naturally stand more in need of forms than other nations, and they naturally respect them less. This deserves most serious attention. Nothing is more pitiful than the arrogant disdain of most of our contemporaries for questions of form; for the smallest questions of form have acquired in our time an importance which they never had before: many of the greatest interests of mankind depend upon them. I think that if the statesmen of aristocratic ages could sometimes contemn forms with impunity, and frequently rise above them, the statesmen to whom the government of nations is now confided ought to treat the very least among them with respect, and not neglect them without imperious necessity. In aristocracies the observance of forms was superstitious; amongst us they ought to be kept with a deliberate and enlightened deference.

Another tendency, which is extremely natural to democratic nations and extremely dangerous, is that which leads them to despise and undervalue the rights of private persons. The attachment which men feel to a right, and the respect which they display for it, is generally proportioned to its importance, or to the length of time during which they have enjoyed it. The rights of private persons amongst democratic nations are commonly of small importance, of recent growth, and extremely precarious—the consequence is that they are often sacrificed without regret, and almost always violated without remorse. But it happens that at the same period and amongst the same nations in which men conceive a natural contempt for the rights of private persons, the rights of society at large are naturally extended and consolidated: in other words, men become less attached to private rights at the very time at which it would be most necessary to retain and to defend what little remains of them. It is therefore most especially in the present democratic ages, that the true friends of the liberty and the greatness of man ought constantly to be on the alert to prevent the power of government from lightly sacrificing the private rights of individuals to the general execution of its designs. At such times no citizen is so obscure that it is not very dangerous to allow him to be oppressed—no private rights are so unimportant that they can be surrendered with impunity to the caprices of a government. The reason is plain: if the private right of an individual is violated at a time when the human mind is fully impressed with the importance and the sanctity of such rights, the injury done is confined to the individual whose right is infringed; but to violate such a right, at the present day, is deeply to corrupt the manners of the nation and to put the whole community in jeopardy, because the very notion of this kind of right constantly tends amongst us to be impaired and lost. . . .

I shall conclude by one general idea, which comprises not only all the particular ideas which have been expressed in the present chapter, but also most of those which it is the object of this book to treat of. In the ages of aristocracy which preceded our own, there were private persons of great power, and a social authority of extreme weakness. The outline of society itself was not easily discernible, and constantly confounded with the different powers by which the community was ruled. The principal efforts of the men of those times were required to strengthen, aggrandize, and secure the supreme power; and on the other hand, to circumscribe individual independence within narrower limits, and to subject private interests to the interests of the public. Other perils and other cares await the men of our age. Amongst the greater part of modern nations, the government, whatever may be its origin, its constitution, or its name, has become almost omnipotent, and private persons are falling, more and more, into the lowest stage of weakness and dependence. In olden society everything was different; unity and uniformity were nowhere to be met with. In modern society everything threatens to become so much alike, that the peculiar characteristics of each individual will soon be entirely lost in the general aspect of the world. It would seem as if the rulers of our time sought only to use men in order to make things great; I wish that they would try a little more to make great men; that they would set less value on the work, and more upon the workman; that they would never forget that a nation cannot long remain strong when every man belonging to it is individually weak, and that no form or combination of social polity has yet been devised, to make an energetic people out of a community of pusillanimous and enfeebled citizens. . . .

Chapter VIII

GENERAL SURVEY OF THE SUBJECT

Before I close forever the theme that has detained me so long, I would fain take a parting survey of all the various characteristics of modern society, and appreciate at last the general influence to be exercised by the principle of equality upon the fate of mankind; but I am stopped by the difficulty of the task, and in presence of so great an object my sight is troubled, and my reason fails. The society of the modern world which I have sought to delineate, and which I seek to judge, has but just come into existence. Time has not yet shaped it into perfect form: the great revolution by which it has been created is not yet over: and amidst the occurrences of our time, it is almost impossible to discern what will pass away with the revolution itself, and what will survive its close. . . .

When I survey this countless multitude of beings, shaped in each other's likeness, amidst whom nothing rises and nothing falls, the sight of such universal uniformity saddens and chills me, and I am tempted to regret that state of society which has ceased to be. When the world was full of men of great importance and extreme insignificance, of great wealth and extreme poverty, of great learning and extreme ignorance, I turned aside from the latter to fix my observation on the former alone, who gratified my sympathies. But I admit that this gratification arose from my own weakness: it is because I am unable to see at once all that is around me, that I am allowed thus to select and separate the objects of my predilection from among so many others. Such is not the case with that almighty and eternal Being whose gaze necessarily includes the whole of created things, and who surveys distinctly, though at once, mankind and man. We may naturally believe that it is not the singular prosperity of the few, but the greater well-being of all, which is most pleasing in the sight of the Creator and Preserver of men. What appears to me to be man's decline, is to His eye advancement; what afflicts me is acceptable to Him. A state of equality is perhaps less elevated, but it is more just; and its justice constitutes its greatness and its beauty. I would strive then to raise myself to this point of the divine contemplation, and thence to view and to judge the concerns of men.

No man, upon the earth, can as yet affirm absolutely and generally, that the new state of the world is better than its former one; but it is already easy to perceive that this state is different. Some vices and some virtues were so inherent in the constitution of an aristocratic nation, and are so opposite to the character of a modern people, that they can never be infused into it; some good tendencies and some bad propensities which were unknown to the former, are natural to the latter; some ideas suggest themselves spontaneously to the imagination of the one, which are utterly repugnant to the mind of the other. They are like two distinct orders of human beings, each of which has its own merits and defects, its own advantages and its own evils. Care must therefore be taken not to judge the state of society, which is now coming into existence, by notions derived from a state of society which no longer exists; for as these states of society are exceedingly different in their structure, they cannot be submitted to a just or fair comparison. It would be scarcely more reasonable to require of our own contemporaries the peculiar virtues which originated in the social condition of their forefathers, since that social condition is itself fallen, and has drawn into one promiscuous ruin the good and evil which belonged to it.

But as yet these things are imperfectly understood. I find that a great number of my contemporaries undertake to make a certain selection from amongst the institutions, the opinions, and the ideas which originated in the aristocratic constitution of society as it was: a portion of these elements they would willingly relinquish, but they would keep the remainder and transplant them into their new world. I apprehend that such men are wasting their time and their strength in virtuous but unprofitable efforts. The object is not to retain the peculiar advantages which the inequality of conditions bestows upon mankind, but to secure the new benefits which equality may supply. We have not to seek to make ourselves like our progenitors, but to strive to work out that species of greatness and happiness which is our own. For myself, who now look back from this extreme limit of my task, and discover from afar, but at once, the various objects which have attracted my more attentive investigation upon my way, I am full of apprehensions and of hopes. I perceive mighty dangers which it is possible to ward off—mighty evils which may be avoided or alleviated; and I cling with a firmer hold to the belief, that for democratic nations to be virtuous and prosperous they require but to will it. I am aware that many of my contemporaries maintain that nations are never their own masters here below, and that they necessarily obey some insurmountable and unintelligent power, arising from anterior events, from their race, or from the soil and climate of their country. Such principles are false and cowardly; such principles can never produce aught but feeble men and pusillanimous nations. Providence has not created mankind entirely independent or entirely free. It is true that around every man a fatal circle is traced, beyond which he cannot pass; but within the wide verge of that circle he is powerful and free: as it is with man, so with communities. The nations of our time cannot prevent the conditions of men from becoming equal; but it depends upon themselves whether the principle of equality is to lead them to servitude or freedom, to knowledge or barbarism, to prosperity or to wretchedness.

ABOUT THE AUTHOR

ALAN RYAN was born in London in 1940 and educated at Oxford University, where he taught for many
years. He was professor of politics at Princeton University from 1988 to 1996, and warden of New College,
Oxford University, and professor of political theory
from 1996 until 2009. He is the author of *The Philosophy
of John Stuart Mill*, *The Philosophy of the Social Sciences*, *J. S. Mill*,
Property and Political Theory, *Bertrand Russell: A Political Life*,
John Dewey and the High Tide of American Liberalism, *Liberal
Anxieties and Liberal Education*, and *On Politics*. He is married
to Kate Ryan and lives in Princeton, New Jersey.